Foundation Stones

6 Principles to Maturity in Christ

Written by:
Dr. Lon and Laurie Stettler

Copyright Page

Hebrew and Greek terms referenced are from James Strong, *The New Strong's Exhaustive Concordance of the Bible* (Nashville, TN: Thomas Nelson Publishers, 1990)

ISBN: 979-8-9936478-0-7

TABLE OF CONTENTS

Dedication

This book is dedicated first to our Lord Jesus Christ, Who through the ministry of the Holy Spirit, opened our eyes to our 'real' identity in Christ. This revelation of our identity, and how to activate that identity, has truly revolutionized both how we view the Lord and view ourselves. What a liberating and victorious way to live!

I, Lon, dedicate this book to my wonderful wife, Laurie, my companion, confidant, and friend. Her support and encouragement has been invaluable in the writing of this book. Her story is very much a part of the message of this book. Laurie graciously co-labors with me in the work of the ministry.

I, Laurie, thank you, Lon, for a lifetime of love, adventures, joy, encouragement, and family.

Introduction

The Lord desires that you become a mature son or daughter. The Father wants to say to you what He told Jesus at the River Jordan: "You are My beloved Son, in You I am well-pleased." The Father was speaking these words over Jesus as He was now a *mature* Son.

Do you aspire to become a mature son or a mature daughter? A mature son or daughter is one who has mastered the milk and is ready for the meat of Christ's Kingdom. To be ready for the meat, let's make sure that you have mastered the elementary principles of the milk of the kingdom. In the pages ahead, you will learn what the scripture means about becoming a mature "son."

We debated on how best to title this book. A very fitting title could have been *From Milk to Meat: Mastering the 6 Principles to Maturity in Christ* based on Hebrews chapter 5. Another was, *From Milk to Steak Dinner: Mastering the 6 Principles to Maturity in Christ* (Lon's favorite!) However, we felt strongly that the concept of "foundation" was key and we chose the current title: *Foundation Stones*: *6 Principles to Maturity in Christ.*

A part of becoming a mature believer includes mastering core *foundation stones* concerning the apostles' teaching. Hebrews chapter 6:1-3 records that there are six principles that constitute the milk of the teachings of the first apostles in order to move on to the meat. We hope to help you understand and apply these six principles.

The doctrines of Christ are the six basic principles or foundation stones upon which our Christian faith is built that are necessary to proceed to maturity. They are:

- Repentance from Dead Works
- Faith in God
- Doctrine of Baptisms
- Laying on of Hands
- Resurrection of the Dead
- Eternal Judgment

Each believer is to put these six principles into his or her Christian life as a core foundation. Once mastered, you will have the prerequisite needed to move on to the solid food or meat of the Christian faith.

In the context of the Kingdom of God, a mature person is one who has mastered the six principles or foundation stones that comprised the apostles' doctrine in the first century church. A mature believer is skilled to teach the word of righteousness. They can discern between good and evil. They know God's voice and ways. Such a mature believer is skilled enough to partake of the meat or solid food in God's word. They know how to use the keys of kingdom authority on behalf of King Jesus.

If your home does not have a sound foundation, it will collapse under pressure. Likewise, if our spiritual foundation is weak, we cannot add more truth and experience to it and become a mature son or daughter. Our admonition is *"go on to perfection, not laying again the foundation of repentance from dead works and of faith toward God, of the doctrine of baptisms, of laying on of hands, of resurrection of the dead, and of eternal judgment"* (Heb. 6:1-3 NKJV). Once you learn the first principles of Christ, it is time to go on to maturity.

From our experience in discipling others over the past several decades, we have noticed that many (if not most) believers we train don't get beyond the first two principles: *repentance from dead works* and *faith in God*. These young believers don't get past the understanding of "dead works" to maintain an enduring faith in (1) who God is for them, (2) the finished work of Christ on their behalf, and (3) their identity as a Christian. They flounder with these first two principles in their experience and don't progress on to the remaining principles of Christ. As a result, they continue as immature believers who still need the milk of the word. They are not skilled in righteousness yet nor are they ready to be a leader.

In Section 1, *Toward Maturity*, we begin with a description of a mature Christian who has mastered the six principles of Christ. In Section 2 entitled, *The Real "You,"* we provide a solid understanding of who you are in Christ as a foundation to master the first two principles – repentance from dead works and faith in God – so you can move on to maturity. The remaining sections present the truths and understandings of each of the six principles or foundation stones.

Section 1

Toward Maturity

Before we learn the six principles or foundation stones of Christ, we believe it is important to frame our learning with the outcome or end-goal of mastering these principles in mind: maturity. *"Therefore, leaving the discussion of the elementary principles of Christ, let us go on to perfection. . ."* (Heb. 6:1a NKJV). The word *perfection* in this verse means mature or complete. The end-goal of learning the apostolic teaching about Christ is to be a mature and complete son or daughter in Christ.

We devote the first chapter of this book to describe what it means to be a mature son or daughter. Certainly it means to understand and apply the six principles of not laying again the foundation of repentance from dead works and of faith in God, of the doctrine of baptisms, of laying on of hands, of resurrection of the dead, and of eternal judgment. But being mature in the Hebrews 6:1 sense means that you come to the level of being "adopted as a son." What does that really mean? Let's unpack this important perspective.

Chapter 1

Becoming a Mature Son

"let us go on to perfection. . . Hebrews 6:1

God wants all of His children to grow up and become mature sons and daughters. The process of maturing is both an invitation and an expectation. Our initial thought may be that to "*go on to perfection*" in this life is not possible. But let's understand how the word "perfection" is being used here. The word *perfection* in Hebrews 6:1 means a state of being mature or complete.

A fully mature person possesses full authority to represent the family name and business. This person is authorized to speak and represent the father in all matters. In the context of the Kingdom of God, a mature person is certainly one who mastered the six principles or foundation stones that comprised the apostles' doctrine. But there is more to being a mature son or daughter.

As a mature person, you also:

- are skilled to teach the word of righteousness
- are able to discern between good and evil
- know God's voice and ways because you are led by Holy Spirit.
- are skilled enough to partake of the meat (solid food) in God's word, and
- know how to use the keys of kingdom authority on behalf of King Jesus.

In your journey to become a mature "son", let's look in scripture at four Greek words for a daughter or son, each depicting a different level of maturity. These words are used to describe various stages of spiritual maturity. Let's do a little vocabulary work. (We are not seeking to overwhelm you with Greek vocabulary but to give you the right perspective!)

- *Nepios* means "no speech" and refers to an infant or baby and appear in these scriptures: 1 Corinthians 3:1 says: *"And I, brethren, could not speak to you as to spiritual men, but as to men of flesh, as to infants in Christ."*

- A *paidion* is a toddler or young child; Matthew 18:4 says, *"Whoever then humbles himself as this child, he is the greatest in the kingdom of heaven."*

- A *teknon* is a child, up to and including a teenager or young adult; immature. Galatians 4:19 says, *"My children, with whom I am again in labor until Christ is formed in you."* 1 John 5:21, *"Little children, guard yourselves from idols."*

- Finally, a *huios* is a fully matured "son." Romans 8:14 says, *"For all who are being led by the Spirit of God, these are sons of God."* Matthew 5:45, *"...so that you may be sons of your Father who is in heaven. . ."*

The last term, *huios*, is the goal the Lord is seeking. Spiritually speaking, *huios* is not a gender term; just as a male can be part of Christ's "bride," females can be a fully mature "son." (In a similar way, Jesus made us a new "man" (*anthropos)* in Ephesians 2:15, which also is not referring to gender, but to mankind or the human race; *anthropos* includes both women and men created in the image of God.)

The Peril of Not Advancing

The audience of the book of Hebrews was learning about the peril of not advancing to maturity as believers. From the tone of the passage in Hebrews 5, the writer seems to be issuing a rebuke to his audience. Hebrews 5:12 – 14 NKJV reads:

> *For though by this time you ought to be teachers* [didaskalos = master], *you need someone to teach you again the first principles of the oracles of God; and you have come to need milk and not solid food.*
>
> *For everyone who partakes only of milk is unskilled* [apeiros = inexperienced] *in the word of righteousness, for he is a babe* [nepios = infant, simple-minded].
>
> *But solid food belongs to those who are of full age* [teleious = mature, full-grown], *that is, those who by reason of use have their senses exercised to discern both good and evil.*

Let this passage be an exhortation to you to step up your growth into spiritual adulthood.

The writer of Hebrews (perhaps the apostle Paul?) uses the analogy of those not advancing in their understanding and skill as ones still needing milk and not ready for solid food. The audience is still babes who have not mastered the basics of the first principles of Christ. Not only are they not mature, they are not even toddlers or young adults, but babes. The writer is warning of the danger of not advancing to the point of mature sons and daughters. They are not yet mature enough to discern between good and evil and, therefore, not ready to be a teacher or leader.

The apostle Paul confronted this same immaturity in the church at Corinth (I Cor. 3:1-3). He could not speak to them as spiritual believers but as carnal believers. They were still being led by their flesh and not consistently by the Spirit. As a result, he could not teach them spiritual meat but still gave them the milk of the Word.

"Positioned" as Mature Sons

It's insightful to learn that in Christ's day, when children matured and had been adequately trained, they were "placed" into "sonship." For this important transition, a public ceremony called a *huiothesia* was held.[1] This word literally means "placed as a son." It was different than a *bar mitzvah* ceremony and normally occurred at 30 years of age. The father of the child would invite members of the community to this event, for it was a public announcement that the child was now a fully mature son with full authority to represent the family name and business, giving him a ring, a robe, and sandals. During the ceremony, the father would announce, "You are My beloved Son (*huios),* in You I am well-pleased." This is why Father God spoke these words at Christ's baptism (Mark 1:11); He was declaring that Christ was fully authorized to speak for Him and conduct His business. It was Christ's *huiothesia*, positioning him as a mature "son."

Isaiah prophesied of Christ, *"For a child will be born to us, a son will be given to us; And the government will rest on His* [the Son's] *shoulders;"* (Is. 9:6). Isaiah later tells us that keys of governmental authority are worn or attached to one's shoulder to lock and unlock, which gives us insight of government keys resting on *"His shoulders"* (see Is. 22:22). Keys of authority on one's shoulder signified "chamberlain authority." Matthew 16:19 tells us that Jesus is, likewise, positioning us as mature sons with chamberlain authority, able to use the keys of kingdom authority to bind and to loose on His behalf.

Huiothesia is usually translated "adoption as sons" in the New Testament (Gal. 4:5; Eph. 1:5). Technically, however, the word isn't saying we are being adopted into God's family. It refers to the above ceremony, stating that as His children, already in the family, we are being positioned or placed into "sonship." Adoption as sons emphasizes spiritual inheritance and identity and applies equally to female as well as male believers. God's

---

[1] Dutch Sheets, *Moving in Greater Authority*, accessed February 13, 2024, https://www.givehim15.com/post/february-13-24

plan is to mature us from spiritual babies to mature sons and daughters, who are qualified to fully represent and speak for Him in our sphere of influence. A fully mature "son" exercises all the rights and privileges of an heir and also possesses *kingdom authority.*

This understanding is important in Romans 8 as well. The chapter tells us that as God's children, we have all the rights, blessings, and privileges of being in His family:

> *"The Spirit Himself testifies with our spirit that we are children* [teknon] *of God, and if children,* [teknon] *heirs also, heirs of God and fellow heirs with Christ, if indeed we suffer with Him so that we may also be glorified with Him"* (Romans 8:16-17, bracket added).

Romans 8 makes an important distinction between children/teenagers (*teknon*) and mature sons, saying that "sons" *(huios)* of God are *led* by His Spirit. *"For all who are being led by the Spirit of God, these are sons (huios) of God"* (Rom. 8:14). Many of God's kids are not yet led by Holy Spirit. Though they have access to His blessings, they are not mature enough to know His voice and ways. Some never grow to this point. Children have rights and benefits; mature sons also possess kingdom authority.

> Mature sons also possess kingdom authority.

Paul further writes in Romans 8:

> *For the anxious longing of the creation waits eagerly for the revealing of the sons* [huios] *of God. . .that the creation itself also will be set free from its slavery to corruption into the freedom of the glory of the children of God.* (Romans 8:19, 21, bracket added)

This passage tells us that creation is groaning and travailing, waiting for the revealing of the "sons" of God - NOT the revealing of His children – but the revealing of "sons."

Christians who are at the child level of maturity cannot bring healing to the earth; only mature sons and daughters, those led by Holy Spirit, can do so. These "sons" of God know His Word and ways, carry His heart, and are led by His Spirit, enabling them to represent Christ. There is no better scripture to describe the impact of possessing our communities than the above passage: mature sons setting creation free to reveal the glory of God. As Christ's church, we

> Only mature sons and daughters, those led by Holy Spirit, can bring healing to the earth.

are to manifest a level of this sonship now, representing His spiritual authority and releasing His healing to a groaning earth.

Let's Apply!

Do you seek to be led by the Spirit? Are you able to hear His voice?

Are you learning the ways of God as a mature "son?"

The spiritual battle we are a part of has always been between "the sons" -- the sons of light and the sons of darkness. When Jesus was explaining the parable of the tares in Matthew 13, Christ called His disciples "sons of the kingdom" and tares as the "sons of the evil one." Similarly, Paul refers to the battle as between the sons of light and the sons of darkness. The battle is not between the members of the Godhead and the devil, in view of the fact that the devil is our enemy, not God's enemy. No, the battle for our families and communities is between the sons of light and sons of darkness.

A Company of Mature "Sons"

God is maturing a company of believers throughout the earth into their "sonship" stage. He wants you to be a part of this company. God has put guardians and managers in your life to govern you into maturity (Gal. 4:2). Your *guardian* is the Holy Spirit and your *managers* are the fivefold ministers (apostles, prophets, pastors, teachers, and evangelists) who grow you into sonship.

> Your guardian is the Holy Spirit and your managers are the fivefold ministers who grow you into sonship.

You are growing in wisdom and knowledge. No longer a spiritual baby or child, you are being matured to a point where you can be trusted with Christ's authority. God gives you a sphere of influence in which you carry his authority to steward for Him in the Kingdom.

As a mature son or daughter, you will bring salvation, healing, and restoration to the needy in your life, teaching them to prosper. Some of you will transform governments, education, economies, medicine, farming, and more. Others of you will be healers of decimated cities and nations (Is. 58:12), delivering the oppressed and downtrodden (Luke 4:18-19). Move in humility, and in power. Operate in love, and release His kingdom authority.

Jesus wants you to be mature and activated as a mature son.

Let's Apply!

God wants to mature you as a son and position you as a mature "son." Are you allowing Him to mature you to take your community?

Let's Internalize and Apply!

1. What does the word *perfection* mean in Hebrews 6:1?

   ____

   ____

2. What does the Greek word *huios* mean?

   ____

   ____

3. What does the Greek term *huiothesia* mean?

   ____

   ____

4. True/False: Adoption as sons emphasizes spiritual inheritance and identity and applies equally to female as well as male believers.

5. True/False: A fully mature "son" exercises all the rights and privileges of an heir and also possesses kingdom authority.

6. True/False: Creation is groaning and travailing, waiting for the revealing of the "sons" of God - NOT the revealing of His "children."

7. The spiritual battle we are a part of has always been between what "sons"?

   ____

   ____

Section 2

The Real "You"

With the end-goal of being "adopted as a mature son" in mind, let's first understand our identity in Christ.

Many believers don't fully understand the first two principles of *repentance from dead works* and *faith in God*. Why? They do not really grasp who they are in Christ. They don't understand how God views them as a new creation in Christ based on the finished work of Christ at Calvary. Nor do they really grasp the freedom of having a clear conscience with God and how to maintain an enduring faith in God. We have found it essential to know your identity as a Christian, based on Christ's finished work for you.

In this section, we will provide you with a clear revelation of who you are in Christ as the foundation for mastering all six of the principles of Christ and move on to maturity.

Chapter 2

One Version of You

We each have a picture in our mind's eye of how we see ourselves. How you perceive yourself is a lens or filter you use as you think about *you*. You have a version of you in your mind. In your journey as a Christian, you probably have learned that some of your perceptions are correct and others are not, which you learn to correct over time. Your view is shaped by experiences over time and the degree to which you have conformed your thinking to what is true about you in scripture.

The place we are going to begin is with your Father's perception of you. Have you ever wondered:

> *How does the Father **see** or view me? Jesus view me? Holy Spirit view me?*
>
> *What do They **think** of me?*
>
> *How do They **talk** to one another about me?*
>
> *How do the angels of heaven **talk** about me?*

The answers to these provocative questions are found in scripture and form our starting point. One of the most important revelations from scripture in the New Testament is the understanding that the three members of the Godhead *only have one version of you in mind – a new man who is born of the Spirit and washed in Jesus' blood!*

The Father, the Son, and Holy Spirit do not see or have two versions of you – the old man and the new man. They do not have double vision. There is only one version of you – your new man -- living in Jesus and learning to be one with Him. While you may hold two versions of yourself –the old and new natures -- the Godhead does not. They only recognize and know you as a new man in Christ. It is the only version of you they know. They are not double-minded about you.

> There is only one version of you – your new man!

The Father sees you in Jesus. Your quality of life in Him is the same as what the Father enjoys with Jesus and Holy Spirit. You are a new creation walking in love with your God, and learning to live in fellowship with Christ. The Father loves you the way He loves Jesus. In fact, He sees Jesus in you. The Holy Spirit, your Helper, loves you the same way He loves the Father and Jesus.

Once you are born-again, the Godhead only sees and knows you as a new creation. You now carry the image of the Son. Jesus put a full layer of Himself -- His personhood and deity -- into you when you were born-again. You now have what we will call a *born-again* spirit. This is what each member of the Godhead sees every day and in every situation when they look at you. They are calling you into your real identity in Christ as a beloved son or daughter.

Hear the Father's words to you:

> *Beloved, We are not seeing two of you...the old man and the new man. We do not have double vision. There is only one of you living in Jesus and learning to be one with Him. We are not in two minds or versions about you. We only speak to your identity as a saint, never as a sinner. We only work on the new you. The old you is dead, so let it rest in peace.*

When Christ was raised from the dead, your old nature was left in the grave and was not resurrected. When Jesus was buried, He took your old nature with Him. When He was raised from the dead, He left your old nature behind in the grave; it was not resurrected. You were resurrected with a new nature in newness of life. The apostle Paul said this very clearly:

> *Therefore if anyone is in Christ, he is a new creature; the old things* [old nature] *passed away; behold, new things* [nature of Christ] *have come. Now all these things are from God.* (2 Corinthians 5:17-18a, bracket added)

This scripture describes a transaction of sorts. The old man was crucified and buried with Christ and the new man in you was raised to newness of life.

The Father only sees one version of you. He sees you only in Christ. God only deals with the new man in us, because Jesus put to death the old man on the cross and left it buried in the grave. Yes, the Father is aware of your old nature but pays no attention to it because it has been put to death and left buried in the grave.

> God only deals with the new man in us, because Jesus put to death the old man on the cross.

You may not know it but you are positionally co-identified with Christ. As Jesus was crucified, you are *co-crucified* with Him because of your close identity with Christ. As Jesus was buried, you are *co-buried* with Him. As Jesus was resurrected, you are *co-resurrected!* As Jesus ascended and was seated at the right hand of the Father in heavenly places, so too you are *co-ascended* and *co-seated* with Christ in heavenly places.[2]

Old Self: Rom. 6:6; Col. 3:9; Eph. 4:22 **New Self**: Col. 3:10; Eph. 4:24

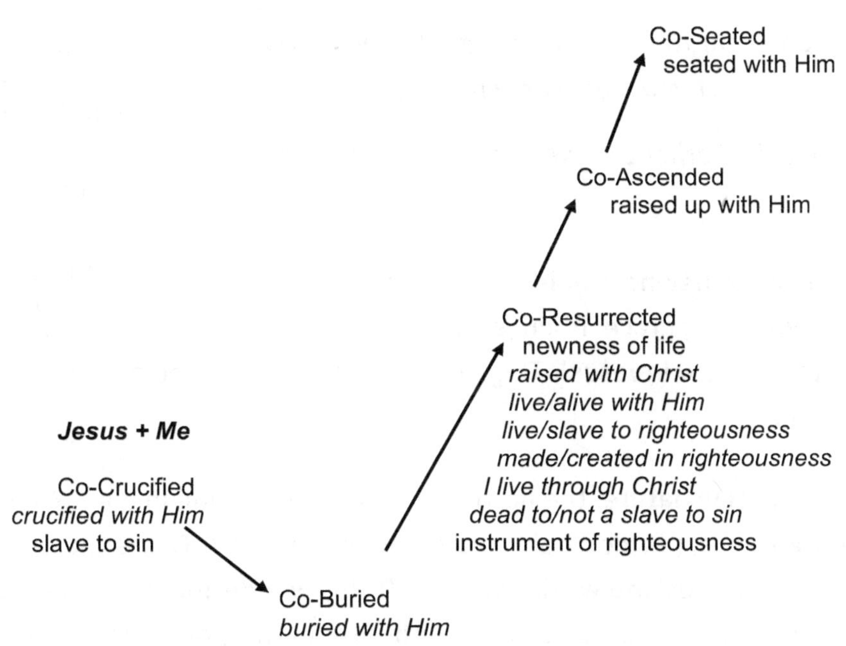

So, when Jesus Christ rose from the dead in newness of Life, none of your old nature was resurrected. It was left behind in the grave. Now the Father only sees the new you in Jesus. The old you is dead.

> None of your old nature was resurrected. It was left behind in the grave.

Listen to the Father's words to you:

When My beloved Son rose from the dead in newness of Life, none of your old nature made it through the resurrection. The old you is dead. It was left behind. We made sure of it.

[2] Here are the scriptural references for your further study. Co-Crucified: Gal. 2:20; Rom. 6:6. Co-Buried: Rom. 6:4; Col. 2:12. Co-Resurrected: Rom. 6:4, 8, 11; I Pet. 2:24; Col. 2:13; Eph. 2:4-5; Eph. 4:24. Co-Ascended: Eph. 2:4-6; Col. 3:1. Co-Seated: Eph. 2:6

When My Son died, so did you. He died for you and He died as you.

When He was buried, He took your old man with Him. When He was raised from the dead, He left your old nature behind. The old man can never be resurrected. It is gone, finished forever. Your new man is Christ in you, giving you His nature.

Let's Discuss!

How can you upgrade your thinking and speaking about yourself to align with the one version that God has about you – as a new man in Christ?

Do you believe what the Father believes and says about you?

> The Father only speaks to you in your identity as a *saint*, never as a *sinner*.

When Jesus rose again to newness of life, who also rose with Him? You! His life, righteousness, grace, holiness, faith, character, and power all belong to you now in Jesus! The Father has redeemed you and recreated you in the image of His Son.

So the *real* you is your new nature, the nature of Jesus Christ living in you. Your *born-again spirit*[3] is as righteous, perfect, holy, and complete as Jesus. This is the only version of you that the Godhead sees and works with. Isn't this wonderful! (We will expand further on what's true about your redeemed spirit later in this book.) Now, the Father speaks to you in your identity as a *saint*, never as a *sinner*. The Godhead only works on the new you. The old you is dead so leave it alone.

God is inviting you to VIEW yourself, THINK about yourself, and TALK about yourself the same way that heaven does. You really cannot afford to think thoughts about yourself that God does not think about you. Likewise, you cannot afford to speak words about yourself that God has not said about you.

> You cannot afford to think thoughts about yourself that God does not think about you.

Your biggest battles are always about your true identity. Your adversary brings assaults against your sonship in Christ and against the Christ living in

[3] We use the term "born-again spirit" to mean the condition of your spirit after you receive Christ and are a new creation; it is our way of distinguishing it from the previous condition of your spirit (old nature, old man) that was spiritually dead.

you. Your adversary does not want you to understand your true identity as you are striving to live from that true identity as a new creation. Your battles become more challenging when you do not clearly understand that, in the courts of heaven, *there is only one version of you – the new man.*

Your soul (especially your mind and conscience) must catch up with the transformation that has occurred in your spirit. If you are like most Christians, you have double-vision – that is, you see yourself as possessing both the old nature and the new nature at the same time. Why? Even though you know that you are a new creation in Christ, you still find yourself defaulting to the old nature and resurrecting your old nature. You still have memories and habits associated with your old nature that need to be replaced. So you live out two versions of yourself. Our goal through this book is to assist you in moving away from living out two versions of yourself and, instead, living out the one version of a new creation in Christ. It's what the Godhead sees and works on.

To catch up to your spirit, the soul part of you (in your mind and heart) must put off the old nature and put on the new nature. The apostle Paul explained this process when he wrote to the Ephesians and the Colossians.

> *. . .you <u>lay aside</u> the old self, which is being corrupted in accordance with the lusts of deceit, and that you be renewed in the spirit of your mind, and <u>put on</u> the new self, which in the likeness of God has been created in righteousness and holiness of the truth.* (Ephesians 4:22b – 24)

> *. . .since you <u>laid aside</u> the old self with its evil practices, and have <u>put on</u> the new self who is being renewed to a true knowledge according to the image of the One who created him.* (Colossians 3:9b-10)

In upcoming chapters we will share several tools to facilitate putting off the old nature and putting on the new one. The Father wants you to see the *real* you – the version of you that He sees because of the finished work of Christ. Understanding and living out of your new nature is essential to mastering the six principles of Christ and growing to maturity.

Let's Internalize and Apply!

1. The Father only has one view of you. What is that view?

____

____

2. Where is your old nature now?

____

____

3. Why does God only deal with the new man in us?

____

____

Chapter 3

Not Modifiable

One of the struggles we often have results from not making a clear distinction between our new nature and our old nature (the old man). The scripture is clear that God through the finished work of Christ put to death our old nature and raised us to newness of life in Christ. The Father knew that our old nature was not modifiable.

When Christ died for you, He killed off the old man because it was not modifiable.

Why did the Father kill off the old man at the cross? Because simply changing your old nature does not work. Father God knew that changing the 'old' you using *behavior modification* does not work. He already showed us that this does not work with the children of Israel consistently failing to modify their heart attitudes and behavior to keep the Law. Your old nature was not modifiable.

Instead, the Father gave you an entirely new nature (Greek: *anthropos* = new mankind) that has never existed before (Eph. 2:15)! Your new nature is the nature of Christ that is magnificent, majestic, supreme, and glorious. In your spirit, you are now a new creation that is remade in righteousness. The Father put you in Christ, and Christ into you, so He could treat you like He treats Jesus! You stand today before the Father as if you were Christ, because Christ stood before the Father as you.

> The Father put you in Christ, and Christ into you, so He could treat you like He treats Jesus!

You now have permission to consider yourself dead to sin and alive unto Him. That is how the Father sees you.

> *Consider yourselves to be dead to sin, but alive to God in Christ Jesus.* Romans 6:11

Why should you consider yourself dead to sin? Because the Father does.

Holy Spirit will teach you the lifestyle of being alive in Him. So when God looks at you, He doesn't see anything wrong, because He killed off all sin and negativity. He's really happy about that now. He is not dealing with your sin because He already dealt with it once and for all (Rom. 6:10; Heb. 7:27; I Pet. 3:18). God does not and has not charged sin to any believer's account for over 2,000 years! Of course, you still will need to repent when the Spirit of God convicts you, but your sin issue was addressed two thousand years ago.

You are no longer a slave to sin. It is no longer your nature. The old nature is dead and at rest in the grave. God does not have a *sin conscious* view of you, because Jesus dealt with sin once and for all. Rather, the Godhead has a *righteousness conscious* view of you made in Their image and likeness. As we will learn, the Lord is working to remove a sin mindset about yourself and replace it with a righteousness mindset and understanding.

Unfortunately, most of us have been trying to resurrect our old nature for so long that we qualify as apostles. We are raising the dead every single day. We raise more corpses from the dead than all the apostles combined! We unknowingly attempt to resurrect our old nature – a dead corpse – as a default response.

You may find yourself asking:

> "I seem to always *default* to the old man rather than my new nature. I unknowingly respond from the flesh rather than from the Spirit. I'm learning Jesus killed off my old man at the cross and left it in the grave. How do I stop going directly to the old man and instead live only in my new nature?

Here's the thing: Even though your old nature was legally (in heaven's court) co-crucified and co-buried with Jesus, your old nature is still present in you. Your flesh nature (soul following the lead of your physical body) will default to it and resurrect it . . . if you allow it. We encourage you to consider yourself dead to sin and alive unto Him. Don't work on your sin; work on your righteousness, your true identity. That's what the Father is doing: upgrading your identity, not your sin.

> Don't work on your sin; work on your righteousness, your true identity.

Let's apply Luke 9:23-24 to what we are learning:

> *"If anyone wishes to come after Me, he must deny himself* [old nature]*, and take up his cross daily and follow Me. For whoever wishes to save his life* [old nature] *will lose it, but whoever loses his life* [old nature] *for My sake, he is the one who will save it.* (brackets added)

Deny your old nature, do not default to it; rather, consider yourself dead to it and live free in Christ. Surrender your will to His will. Ask Jesus to fill you with the Holy Spirit so you display the fruit of the Spirit. Christ came to free you from the trappings of the old nature, so stay free in Christ!

As we continue through this book, you will learn ways to put off the old man so you can become the new man. For now, please know your new man is Christ in you, giving you His nature. Your new man has all the things you need to walk with God. It is built into Jesus, who is in you.

God is not practicing behavior modification on your old man in an attempt to upgrade your old nature. But religion is.

Religion is about trying to change the behavior of your old nature. But God is not practicing behavior modification on you. He is not upgrading your old nature. He already killed off your old man and placed it in the grave. Behavior modification does not work on a dead corpse.

God is not calling out your behavior, He is calling you up into your identity in Christ.

God gave you a new Christ nature and now reprograms your mind with the mind of Christ so you reflect the ways of the new man rather than resort to habits of the old man. You do not become a new person by changing your behavior. You became the new man when you received Christ into your spirit.

God is not calling out your behavior, He is calling you up into your identity in Christ.

Each member of the Godhead always speaks to you according to your true identity in Christ. They only see one version of you. They see you as a *learner*, not a failure or a loser. Anything less would be an insult to the finished work of Christ.

God only sees you as a *learner*, not a failure or a loser.

Let's Internalize and Apply!

1. The Father put you in Christ, and Christ in you, so that He could treat you like whom?

   ____

   ____

2. What happens in your life when you default to your old nature instead of the new man?

   ____

   ____

3. Why is the Godhead not practicing behavior modification on you?

   ____

   ____

4. T/F – God is always speaking to you from your identity in Christ.

Chapter 4

His Doing vs My Doing

So far you have learned that God has, sees, and knows only one version of you -- your new man. You have also learned that your old nature is not modifiable by religion or your efforts.

Still, through our church experience we feel the pressure to modify our old nature through our works or efforts. God changes our inside and works out, while we often try to change the outside to affect the inside. We confuse or blur *His Doing* versus *My Doing*. The scripture is clear that it is *"by **His doing** you are in Christ Jesus"* (I Cor. 1:30a).

Your adversary wants you to mix up your *being* with your *doing*. Because all your sins are completely forgiven (based on *His Doing*), there is nothing you can add (My Doing) to cause God to love and fully accept you more. Be watchful, for your adversary would like for you to think that it was, say, 90% *His Doing*, and 10% *My Doing*. No, it has always been *100% His Doing*.

Let's try to clarify biblically what our perspective should be.

Question: *Does the Father accept you?*

Answer: This is the wrong question. The real question should be: Is the Father satisfied with the finished work of Jesus? Ephesians 1:6 NKJV says you are *"accepted in the Beloved"*, and Romans 15:7 NASB states *"accept one another, just as Christ also accepted us to the glory of God."* So the answer is: To the *extent* that God the Father is *satisfied* with and accepts Jesus' finished work, He is *satisfied with me*! In my born-again spirit, it is 100% His doing, and 0% my doing.

My Doing	His Doing
0%	100%

The original question (*Does the Father accept you*?) puts the attention on *My Doing* when the real issue is on *His Doing* based on His finished work. Our adversary deceptively keeps trying to move our attention to the *My Doing* column rather than keeping it on the *His Doing* column, putting the attention on self rather than Jesus.

We must keep the focus on the *His Doing* side of the chart. Now, in your born-again spirit, the Father is 100% satisfied with you based on the finished work of Christ.

A few more examples:

Question: *Is God pleased with you?*

To the extent that God the Father is *fully pleased* with Jesus' finished work, He is *fully pleased with you*!

Question: *Are you holy?*

To the extent that *Jesus is holy* in the eyes of His Father, you are holy in the eyes of your heavenly Father in your born-again spirit. As a Christian, you first must *be* holy (I Pet. 1:16) in your born-again spirit, before you can *live* holy (I Pet. 1:15).

One final question: *Are you righteous?*

To the *extent that Jesus is righteous* in the eyes of His Father, you are righteous in the eyes of your Heavenly Father.

We hope you are learning the correct sentence stem to answer these questions: *To the extent that Jesus is __________ in the eyes of the Father, I am ________ in the eyes of my Father.*

As Jesus is NOW, so also are You in this World!

> *. . .as He is* [now], *so also are we* [in our born-again spirit] *in this world.* **(**I John 4:17, brackets added)

As Jesus Christ is *now*, so are you in your born-again spirit. Let that sink in. Your born-again spirit is—right now—as *perfect, mature*, and *complete* as Jesus Himself. Your born-again spirit is as perfect and complete as it'll ever be throughout all eternity. When God looks at you, He sees your born-again spirit that is as *righteous* and *holy* as Jesus.

To begin to see what has transpired in your born-again spirit, let's take a look at some of the truths about you.

<u>As Jesus Christ is Now. . .</u>		**<u>So Am I in my Born-Again Spirit</u>**
To the extent that Jesus is *righteous*. . .		I am *righteous* (Eph. 4:24; II Cor. 5:21)
To the extent that Jesus is *holy*. . .		I am *holy* (Eph. 4:24; I Cor. 3:17)
To the extent that Jesus is *totally accepted* by His Father. . .		I am *totally accepted* (Rom. 15:7) by my heavenly Father
To the extent that Jesus is *well pleasing* to His Father. . .		I am *well pleasing* to my Father (Matt. 3:17; Mark 1:11)
As Jesus now is *perfect, complete,* and *mature*. . .		I am *perfect, complete, and mature* (Heb. 10:14; 12:23)
As Jesus is *crowned with honor and glory*. . .		I am *crowned with honor and glory* (Heb. 2:7)
To the extent that Jesus was *approved* by His Father. . .		I am *approved* (I Thess. 2:4)
As Jesus was *chosen* by His Father. . .		I am *chosen* (Col. 3:12; I Peter 2:9)

Remember, we are looking at how God our heavenly Father is viewing you. When the Father looks at you in your born-again spirit, He sees Jesus! It's the only version of you that He recognizes and knows. The more you learn about who you are in your born-again spirit, the more you will discover about Jesus. Conversely, the more you learn about Jesus, the more you will discover about who you are in your spirit.

Let's Discuss!

Using the following sentence stem. . .

> *To the extent that Jesus is _________ in the eyes of the Father, I am _______ in the eyes of my Father.*

. . .what are three statements you can tell yourself when you need to flip the script in your mind and remind yourself of who God says you are?

Chapter 5

Jesus in the Mirror

You were created to look and be like God. The Psalmist said you are fearfully and wonderfully made.

> *Then God said, 'Let Us make man in Our image, according to Our likeness. . . God created man in His own image.* Genesis 1:26–27

> *. . .I am fearfully* [to stand in awe of] *and wonderfully made.* (Psalm 139:14b, brackets added)

You are *amazing*.

You are more *amazing* and *awesome* than you know.

Can you picture it? The Creator of the universe, who created you, takes a couple of steps back and looks at you and says, "Wow, you are awesome!" He stands in awe of you, His creation.

God *created* us, and now *recreated* us (you are now a 'new creation'), in such a way that we provide an accurate reflection of His glory back to Him and onto the world.

We invite you to look in God's mirror to see what He sees. You will look a whole lot like Jesus!

Each one of us is unique, and we were created to provide the most complete mirror image of God on earth. We are to reflect "Jesus in the Mirror!"

Identity Formation

Miles McPherson points out that we have two competing mirrors that we look at that affect our identity formation on the inside. There is a right mirror and a wrong mirror to view.[4]

---

[4] Miles McPherson, *God in the Mirror* (Grand Rapids, MI: Baker Publishing Group, 2013), 7-8, 13-32

The Right Mirror, God's Word. As a believer in Jesus, you now have an *I AM factor* from God – your individual uniqueness – which positions you above all living things to be in relationship with God. You look into your spiritual mirror, God's Word, to see who you are in your born-again spirit which looks like Jesus -- which Miles calls your *I AM factor*.

Your *I AM factor* reflects the *I AM-ness of God,* your 'God image'.

> A mistake is an event; it is not your identity!

I am fearfully and wonderfully made. Psalm 139:14

And You crown him with glory and majesty! Psalm 8:5

Don't let anyone take your crown!

God has given you a new name – a "Christian". That new name reflects your I AM factor, the 'real you.' This new name has many facets which we will discover shortly.

Jesus, the Great I AM, has put His nature in our human spirit, and recreated our *I AM-ness*, the 'real me.'

The result is you will develop a 'righteousness consciousness' of yourself as you *own* the I Am-ness that you see in this spiritual mirror. You will see yourself as a *saint*, and not a *sinner.* A 'righteousness consciousness' is the gold standard you are to pursue.

The Wrong Mirror. The problem is we often have an inaccurate understanding of our new self as a Christian; we're not sure what is the 'real me'. Miles calls this inaccurate view our *I AM imposter.*

Your *I AM imposter* is an inaccurate or incomplete understanding of who you are as a Christian. It is a deception; a counterfeit version or knockoff of who God has created you to be.

In the natural your thoughts (about you) are not God's thoughts about you. For God's thoughts about you and me are higher than our natural thoughts. You must look into God's spiritual mirror to see what God thinks about you – how God created you and sees you.

Another way you develop this wrong understanding of yourself as a Christian is when you try to create a *name* for yourself separate from God – trying to create or find your significance, worth, and value, outside of God. Singer Frank Sinatra sang a famous song, *I Did It My Way*. Have you ever tried to create a name for yourself – apart from your relationship with God? How did that turn out?

Mistakes, Labels, and Lies

You are also looking in the wrong mirror when you think your identity is defined by the *mistakes* you've made, or the *labels* others have put on you, or the *lies* the Enemy has tried to put upon you. Together, these make up our I AM imposter.

Have you ever made a *mistake* like offended someone with your words; or yelled at your friend, spouse or child in anger; or did something disrespectful; or walked out on a relationship. A mistake is an event; it is not your *identity*! Refuse to be a prisoner of your past. A mistake is a life lesson, not a life sentence.

Or perhaps you have believed the *labels* that others have spoken over you: you're just average; or inferior; not capable; have an addiction; or you're a loser.

Maybe you have believed some of the *lies* the enemy has whispered in your ear, such as you don't have what it takes; you're not talented or special; you don't measure up.

And then there's the *negative self-talk* that doesn't let God get a Word in edgewise! If you don't silence those competing voices, they'll eventually deafen you. Which voice are you listening to?

A lie, a label, or a mistake can become the basis of the devil's accusation against you. Each of these are an assault against your sonship, your identity in Christ. However, when the enemy hears you assert your identity in Christ by rejecting those accusations, he no longer sees only you; he sees Jesus!

If you dwell on any of these falsehoods too long, you begin to believe them and identify with them, and you think of them as your name. When this happens, they create a wrong mental image on the inside. If you're not careful, the wrong image (from labels, mistakes, lies, negative self-talk) will become deeply entrenched emotionally in your heart and very difficult to overcome. A name is a powerful thing.

If you think any of these are your identity, you are looking in the *wrong* mirror. Continuing to look in the wrong mirror will result in you seeing yourself as a sinner, having a '*sin consciousness*'.

As a Christian, you are NOT

- what your *mistakes* say you are
- the *labels* people put upon you
- the *lies* the devil says about you

- who you've *tried to create* yourself to be

You *are who God says you are – deeply loved, completely forgiven, highly valued!*

What you may have done is *not* who you are. Your actions or wrong thinking do not define your identity in Christ. What God has said about you, and provided through Jesus Christ, defines your identity.

Let's Discuss!

What images do you have in your mind of who you are that are the result of looking in the wrong mirror – your mistakes?

Labels from others?

Lies of the enemy?

A name you've tried to create for yourself?

Your actions or wrong thinking do not define your identity in Christ. What God has said about you, and provided through Jesus Christ, defines your identity.

An Identity You Cannot Lose

Your God-given identity, which is in your born-again spirit, is something that you *cannot lose.* If something can be lost, then it is not your identity.

Too often we base our identity and self-worth on our:

- appearance
- talents and abilities
- smarts
- strength
- career success

But you can lose each one of these. Remember: *if you can lose it, it is not your real identity.*

Your God-given identity is based on *who God says you are* in the Bible, God's *spiritual mirror,* and not based on your appearance, or your talents/abilities, or your smarts, or your strength, or your successes.

You are who God says you are and you cannot lose it! The caveat is that you must live out the Christian life and ensure that you maintain your identify in Christ. Just as Adam and Eve forfeited their intimate relationship with God, so can you. Don't reject your great salvation resulting in your name being erased out of the Lamb's Book of Life (Rev. 3:5; Heb. 10:26, 29).

You were created to *wear the name* that you have been given – a name that reflects your I AM-ness from your Creator. Rather than make a name for yourself, wear the name that you have been given.

> *I have called you by name; you are Mine*! Isaiah 43:1
>
> *I will give him. . . a new name. . . I will write on him the name of My God. . .* Revelation 2:17; 3:12

Notice that God *exclusively* gets to name us, and not we ourselves or others (labels).

You not only bear God's image but you know His voice. Learning to hear the voice of God is key to discovering your destiny and fulfilling your potential. Know your true identity. When you know who you are, it doesn't matter who you are not. Don't focus on what you aren't, focus on what you are!

Is God's voice the *loudest* voice in your life?

That's the question.

If the answer is no, that's the problem.

Chronic noise may be the greatest impediment to your spiritual growth. When your life gets loud, with noise filling every frequency, you lose your sense of being. And when your schedule gets busy, you lose your sense of balance.

Pursue the truth about you which originates from your born-again spirit (which has access to the mind of Christ), and not from your natural mind. God's Word tells you what is true about your born-again spirit.

So where do you see yourself on the continuum below? Place an "X" on the continuum line below.

'I AM Factor' Continuum

I AM	I AM
Imposter____	Factor

Let's trade in your *I AM imposter* for your true *I AM factor*! Run toward your God-given destiny rather than away from it! Wear the name you have been given!

Let's Discuss!

How do you walk away from your "I AM imposter" so that you wear the name you've been given?

What image do you see in the mirror? Which mirror are you looking at – I AM imposter? Your God image?

How can you go from looking in the I AM imposter mirror (your mistakes, labels from others, lies from enemy) and flip the script so that you look more intently at your I AM factor – the 'real' you?

Let's Internalize and Apply!

1. What is meant by your "I AM factor"?

   ____

   ____

2. How does it differ from the "I AM imposter?"

   ____

   ____

3. How do you move from the "I AM imposter" to the "I AM factor?"

   ____

   ____

4. Have you ever tried to create a name for yourself – apart from your relationship with God -- trying to find significance, worth, and value separate from God? How did that turn out? Who has the exclusive right to give you a name? How should you respond?

Chapter 6

What's True about the One Version of You

But we have this treasure in earthen vessels. . . 2 Corinthians 4:7a

Since the Lord only sees and talks about one version of you as a new creation or a new man in Christ, it is instructive to learn a little more about what is true about this version of you.[5] Jesus is the Treasure who lives in you, so your born-again spirit is a "treasure" within you. Let's learn a little more about what's true about you as a new creation.

The spirit part of you was instantly and completely transformed when you were born-again. Let's drill down a little more and learn some key truths about your born-again spirit – the one version that the Father sees and talks about. After all, He is the one who recreated you through Christ Jesus so you probably want to learn more about what this means.

Truth #1: At this very moment, your born-again spirit is as perfect and complete as it'll ever be throughout all eternity.

Did you know that you are *perfect* and *complete* in your born-again spirit? The writer of Hebrews tells us that through the finished work of Christ, the spirit of the righteous are made *perfect* (Heb.12:23). Your born-again spirit is sealed to keep out the impurities and evil, and seal in your new nature -- which is righteous, holy, perfect, complete.[6] When you were born-again, your spirit was encased – vacuum packed – by the Holy Spirit for preservation. Your born-again spirit retains the holiness and purity of Christ – and will for eternity!

As a Christian, when you sin, that sin cannot enter into your spirit but it can have a negative impact on your soul and body. Sin, if left unconfessed, can have an oppressive effect on your soul and ultimately on your body. It will also weigh heavily upon your spirit and fellowship with God and with other people.

---

[5] See 2 Corinthians 5:17; Galatians 6:15; Ephesians 2:15

[6] See 2 Corinthians 5:21; Ephesians 4:24; Hebrews 12:23; Colossians 2:10

When you enter heaven, you will not get a new spirit upon your arrival there, nor will your spirit need to be matured, or completed, or cleansed. Your spirit (the "new" man) down here is as perfect and complete as it'll ever be throughout all eternity.

Truth #2: Your born-again spirit is—right now—as *perfect, mature*, and *complete* as Jesus Himself.

You are a born-again spirit, you have a soul, and you live in a body. You are a newly created person who did not exist before – a new kind of mankind that is – right now – as perfect, mature, and complete as Jesus Himself. This should not be surprising because you received the spirit of Christ, God's holy Son, into your spirit when you were born again. You are as perfect and complete as you will ever be throughout all eternity.

The Greek word for a new *man* in Ephesians 2:15 is *anthropos*, which means a new kind or race of man. You are now a member of a new race of people – the *saints* race, or the church race. You are part of a newly created people who did not exist before – a new superior kind of mankind now seated at the right hand of the Father. As a member of the saints race of people, you are superior to the first man, Adam. While Adam was created in innocence, you have been created in *righteousness*! And while Adam had authority and dominion over the earth, you have authority in *both* heaven and earth.

You are as clean, holy, and pure as Jesus himself in your born-again spirit. So continue to live in freedom and repent of anything that defiles your body and your soul.

> *. . . as He* [Jesus] *is* [now], *so also are we in this world.* (I John 4:17, brackets mine)

Let's Discuss!

Your born-again spirit is as righteous, holy, perfect, and compete as Jesus. How difficult is it for you to believe that statement?

As Jesus is now, so also are you in your born-again spirit. What will you do to internalize and embrace this truth?

Unfortunately, you (should we say *we*) still have some "old data" from our "old nature" (wrong self-image, values, mannerisms) still lingering in our thinking, and we try to impose it upon our "new man" and it simply does not work. You must completely put off the old self with its memories and habits and reprogram your soul with the "new man" of your born-again spirit.

God's spiritual mirror, His Word, perfectly reflects your born-again spirit, the 'real' you, which looks a lot like Jesus!

Truth #3: When you sin, it does not originate from your born-again spirit. Your born-again spirit does NOT participate when you sin.

Your born-again spirit is *not* capable of committing sin. Read the following scriptures closely.

> *Whoever has been born of God does not sin, for His* [Christ's] *seed remains in him; and he cannot sin, because he has been born of God.* (I John 3:9, NKJV, bracket added)
>
> *We know that no one who is born of God sins; but He* [Christ] *who was born of God keeps him, and the evil one does not touch him.* (I John 5:18, bracket added)
>
> ". . .*as He* [Christ] is [now], *so also are we in this world.*" (I John 4:17)
>
> . . .*for God cannot be tempted by evil, and He Himself* [in your born-again spirit] *does not tempt anyone.* (James 1:13, brackets mine)

When your *soul (mind and will) agrees with your spirit*, you release and experience the *life* of God. The Christian life, by design, is intended to be a life of complete *dependence* on the Lord. When you follow the lead of your spirit, you release life, and not sin. This is where God wants us to live and walk. You live the crucified life (rejecting the flesh with its passions and desires) which enables you to walk in the Spirit, be led by the Spirit, and live in the Spirit. Said another way, when you walk in the Spirit, you will not carry out the desires of the flesh. You are walking in love, faith, wisdom, and as a child of Light. You are allowing your body to be the temple of the Holy Spirit that Christ wants it to be.[7]

> When your *soul agrees with your spirit*, you release and experience the *life* of God.

However, when you choose to live *independent* of the Lord, your *soul agrees with your body* or flesh (apart from your spirit). This closes the valve of the supernatural flow of life from your spirit (and the Holy Spirit within) and the ultimate result will be sin. When you give in to temptation and sin, it originates from your flesh (soul + body), and not from your born-again spirit. The Lord

[7] Galatians 2:20; 5:16, 18, 25; Ephesians 5:2, 8, 15; I Corinthians 6:19

wants you to draw from the Spirit within you, but instead, you yield to your flesh nature causing sin to become active or "alive" (Rom. 7:9). The apostle Paul makes it clear that our tussle is between the new nature in your born-again spirit and your fleshly desires.[8] It is not between your new nature and your old nature (the basis of two versions of yourself), as Jesus did not resurrect your old nature from the grave. Your old nature is dead and in the grave, so leave it alone. When you give in to your carnal desires and impulses, you no longer walk in the freedom for which Christ set you free (Gal. 5:1).

As a Christian walking in the flesh (as a carnal Christian), you begin to walk like a lost person with your understanding darkened, and you separate yourself from the flow of the life of God within you. Your thinking will become dominated by your passions and desires and not by the Spirit. This darkened understanding negatively affects you, your relationships, and your fellowship with God.

We all have a natural inclination to look in the wrong mirror, don't we, which results in wrong thinking and our adopting a wrong understanding of our identity. We return to thinking there are two versions of us and not just the new version of the new creation in Christ. When this occurs, we are dominated by what we can see, taste, hear, smell, and feel instead of God's Word. As a result, the flow of life from our born-again spirit stays turned off.

When you fail or sin (and we all occasionally do), you may think that God the Father is looking at your sin, but He is really looking at the new you, the 'real' you that is created in righteousness and holiness. Remember, the Father only sees one version of you, the new man (*anthropos*).

Why not develop a supernatural inclination to renew your mind and believe God's Word, so that your soul will agree with what has already transpired in your spirit?

When you sin, confess it right away! If you continue to sin, the love of God is not motivating your heart. Continuing to live in sin gives inroads for the devil to work in your life, violates unity and oneness with the Lord, and enslaves you once again. Thankfully, the Holy Spirit guides you to repent and not to repeat that sin in the future!

---

[8] See the tussle between the Spirit and flesh in Galatians 5:16-17, 24-25; Romans 7:6-14, I Corinthians 3:1-3

To summarize, your born-again spirit is *not* capable of sinning nor does sin originate from your spirit. As Jesus is NOW, so am I in this world – righteous, holy, perfect, and complete! This is not an excuse to sin, but should motivate you to stay pure in your Christian life!

Let's Discuss!

We learned that our born-again spirit is not capable of committing sin. How will you change your thinking so you see yourself as God the Father sees the 'real' you?

How Do You See Yourself?

Respond to this statement:

True or False: "I am a sinner saved by grace."

How you answer this statement tells a great deal about how you see yourself.

If you answer TRUE. . .

then as a Christian, you still see yourself as a *sinner*, having a *sin-consciousness* understanding of who you are. You still have an *inaccurate* understanding of your *I AM-ness.*

As a reminder, God only sees one version of you, the new man. He only has a righteousness view of you and doesn't see you as a sinner, but as a *saint.* He sees you as a *learner*, and not a loser or a failure. You need to see yourself the same way.

If you answer FALSE. . .

then you are seeing yourself with a *righteousness-consciousness,* and you are beginning to have an accurate understanding of your *I AM-ness.*

> God sees you as a saint, not as a sinner. He sees you as a learner, and not a loser or a failure.

We might correct the statement this way (the way God sees you now!):

"I ~~am~~ *was* a sinner saved by grace; *now, I am a saint."*

You now stand on *righteousness-ground*, and no longer on condemnation-ground!

God sees the 'real you' (your born-again spirit) as *righteous, holy, perfect,* and *complete* as Jesus; therefore, you should as well.

The goal is to develop a *righteousness* consciousness where you no longer see yourself as a sinner (with a sin consciousness). Rather, you rightly see yourself as a righteous saint. (The term "saint" is a very frequent term for Christians in the New Testament.) You honestly and genuinely can say:

> "I no longer see myself as a sinner, but as a saint. . . who occasionally sins."

God does not see you as a 'sin' consciousness person; He sees you as having a 'righteous' nature, since that is how He has recreated you! That's the gold standard.

Let's Internalize and Apply!

1. As a Christian, you are a born-again spirit, you have a soul, and you live in a body. So what is the 'real you'?

   ____

   ____

2. When God the Father looks at you, what does He see?

   ____

   ____

3. What is the difference between having a *sin-consciousness* and a *righteousness consciousness*? How can you move to having a righteousness consciousness, the gold standard?

   ____

   ____

4. When you sin (and we all do occasionally), does your born-again spirit participate?

   ____

   ____

5. True/False: The Father has a righteousness view of you and only sees you as a *saint,* and never a sinner.

6. True/False: The members of the Godhead see you as a *learner*, and not a loser or a failure.

Section 3

The *Repentance from Dead Works* Principle

"not laying again a foundation of repentance from dead works. . ." Hebrews 6:1

"how much more will the blood of Christ. . .cleanse your conscience from dead works to serve the living God? Hebrews 9:14

Father God wants you to have a clear conscience before Him and others. To live with a good conscience requires repentance from dead works that is coupled with faith in God. A good conscience is a two-sided coin.

Repentance from our dead works – our efforts to please God – is required to receive His forgiveness of our sins so that we experience a clear conscience. Repentance from dead works is fully experienced when you feel the love of the Father without any sense of condemnation from God, from the devil, or from yourself.

In Chapter 7, *Winning in the Courtroom of Heaven*, you will learn about the spiritual context where repentance occurs.

In Chapter 8, *Repentance from Dead Works,* you will learn about the term *repentance* and then about what *dead works* means.

In Chapter 9, *The Completeness of Forgiveness*, you will learn about the completeness of the Father's forgiveness for you. Not understanding the completeness of forgiveness, you will not feel really forgiven and you will return and repent of those same things again and again.

In Chapter 10, *The Gift of a Good Conscience*, you will learn how to maintain a clear conscience and fully accept your identity in Christ.

In Chapter 11, *"Give Me Back My Stuff,"* you will learn how to return to a good conscience when such things as negativity, shame, guilt, and anxiety get in the way of a good conscience before God.

Chapter 7

Winning in the Courtroom of Heaven

To understand the first two principles – *repentance from dead works* and *faith in God* – in a more complete way, it is helpful to know how they function or operate in the spirit realm. The Bible places prayer in general, and repentance and confession in particular, in a courtroom or judicial setting in the spirit realm. In Heaven, there are many different courts that operate (Zech. 3:7). We are not told how many courts there are or their purpose, but it seems plausible that there are different courtrooms set up for different spheres or jurisdictions on the earth.

We do know that the courts of Heaven are *legal places* in the spirit realm in which we can operate. Perhaps you may not have thought of repentance, confession, and forgiveness as something that occurs in the courtroom of Heaven, but it is the case. Repentance that results in forgiveness is a legal transaction that happens in a courtroom in the spirit realm. We gain victory first in the spiritual realm and that affects the physical realm.

Who and what speaks for you in the Courts of Heaven? We have great news for you! Hebrews 12:24 records that the shed blood of Christ *"speaks better things"* about you before the Judge of all. The blood of Jesus answers every accusation against you. Jesus, who is at the right hand of God, always lives to make intercession for you.[9] He speaks for you as your advocate and defense attorney.

First the Courtroom, then the Battlefield

In Scripture, the place of the initial victory is in a courtroom and not on a battlefield. The first place of prayer and repentance should be in the courtroom of Heaven. It is there that we must first win our verdicts before going out to win on the battlefield.

> Jesus never pictures prayer in a battlefield context; He placed prayer in a courtroom or judicial setting.

The first thing we must do to step into the courts of Heaven is to get off of the battlefield. We must gain legal victory through repentance before we run to the battle. We are in a conflict with our adversary, but it is a legal one. Jesus never pictures

[9] See Romans 8:34; Hebrews 7:25

prayer in a battlefield context; He placed prayer in a courtroom or judicial setting. The verdict from the court is the legal "wrestling," and putting the Judge's "not guilty" verdict into place is the battlefield part. The proceedings in the courtroom always come before the victory on the battlefield.

The problem is that many Christians believe that when they pray they are on a battlefield. They rush into a conflict without securing a verdict from Heaven. This is a critical mistake that has caused us to experience defeat, chaos, and backlash from our adversary. We rush into places of prayer only to see things get worse rather than better. This is because we stir things up on the battlefield without first having established a legal precedent to be there. We must first get off the battlefield and into the courtroom.

The proceedings in the courtroom always come before the victory on the battlefield.

Let's Apply!

Has it been your practice to go onto the battlefield to secure a victory before first going to the courts of Heaven? If so, what will you do to reverse this practice?

Once an issue is settled in Heaven, things will change in your life. It takes some legal wrangling to set this in place but once it is done, we can march onto the battlefield and win every time. Go to the third heaven and get favorable verdicts in the courts of Heaven before going to the battlefield in the second heaven. We have the best lawyer and Advocate – Jesus! And better yet, His Father is the Judge. The odds are in your favor with this Judge and your Lawyer, as long as you follow the proper protocol: repent and apply the cleansing blood of Christ to your life first.

We pray the prayer of repentance in the courts of Heaven, as it were, to eliminate the adversary's right to function in our life. Your adversary can only hinder you because he has a legal right to do so.

For context, there are three heavens referred to in scripture. The *first* heaven is the physical heaven, what our physical eyes see. The *second* heaven is the realm where spiritual activity takes place, the work of both angels and demons. It is the realm of principalities and powers and is where spiritual warfare takes place.[10]

The *third* heaven is the spiritual layer above the other two heavens. This is the highest realm in both location and authority. It is the residence of God, the place where His throne is located, as well as the Courts of Heaven. It is the place where Jesus ascended

[10] See Ephesians 6:12; 2 Corinthians 10:4-5

after His resurrection and the eternal home of the saints. Our third heaven authority originates from the position of being seated above all, with Christ in heaven. You are a third-heaven creation operating in third-heaven revelation with the capacity of functioning in third-heaven authority.[11]

The Courts of Heaven

The prophet Daniel saw a glimpse of the Courts of the third heaven in operation. Daniel 7:9-10 unveils the judicial system of heaven.

> *I kept looking*
> *Until thrones were set up,*
> *And the Ancient of Days took His seat;*
> *His vesture was like white snow*
> *And the hair of His head like pure wool.*
> *His throne was ablaze with flames,*
> *Its wheels were a burning fire.*
> *A river of fire was flowing*
> *And coming out from before Him;*
> *Thousands upon thousands were attending Him,*
> *And myriads upon myriads were standing before Him;*
> *The court sat,*
> *And the books were opened.*

Daniel beheld the Father as the Ancient of Days ruling over the courts of Heaven. He is the One who renders decisions from this Court that alter life on Earth. When this Court sets a decision in place, there is no appealing or altering it.

Later in Daniel 7:22, 26-27, we see verdicts of the court of Heaven against the kingdom of darkness.

> *Until the Ancient of Days came and judgment was passed in favor of the saints of the Highest One, and the time arrived when the saints took possession of the kingdom.*

---

[11] See 2 Corinthians 12:2; Ephesians 2:6; Colossians 1:16

> *But the court will sit for judgment, and his* [the devil's] *dominion will be taken away, annihilated and destroyed forever.*
>
> *Then the sovereignty, the dominion and the greatness of all the kingdoms under the whole heaven will be given to the people of the saints of the Highest One; His kingdom will be an everlasting kingdom, and all the dominions will serve and obey Him.*

In this passage, the arrogance and rebellion of the devil and his workers are judged and destroyed by courtroom verdicts of the Judge of all. Applying this protocol to you and me, when we repent in the context of the court of Heaven, we are set free from demonic interference that previously affected us. Notice that one verdict from this Court moves the saints (you and me) from defeat to dominion. This all occurred because of a single verdict or decision from this Court.

It's in the courts of Heaven that you will see victory claimed for you and your family. This Court is the place where you make your case that allows divine decisions to be rendered by the Father, the Righteous Judge on your behalf. This is the place where you operate in authority.

Other passages which show a heavenly courtroom in session include: The court with other divine beings participating in the discussion with God as described by the prophet Micaiah to kings Jehoshaphat and Ahab (I Kings 22: 19-23), and the court of Heaven in operation as the sons of God and Satan were brought before the court regarding Job (Job 1:6-12; 2:1-6).

Jesus actually placed prayer in a judicial setting, and not on a battlefield.

Prayer is Placed in a Judicial Setting

One of the reasons we know we have influence in the Courts is because Jesus actually placed prayer in a judicial setting, and not on a battlefield. In Luke 18, Jesus told a story or parable of a widow coming before an unjust judge. An adversary had a legal case against her. Through her persistent presentation of her case, the judge gave her a right verdict.

> *Now He was telling them a parable to show that at all times they ought to pray and not to lose heart, saying, "In a certain city there was a judge who did not fear God and did not respect man. There was a widow in that city, and she kept coming to him, saying, 'Give me legal protection from my opponent.' For a while he was unwilling; but afterward he said to himself, 'Even though I do not fear God nor*

respect man, yet because this widow bothers me, I will give her legal protection, otherwise by continually coming she will wear me out.' " And the Lord said, "Hear what the unrighteous judge said; now, will not God bring about justice for His elect who cry to Him day and night, and will He delay long over them? I tell you that He will bring about justice for them quickly. However, when the Son of Man comes, will He find faith on the earth?" (Luke 18:1-8)

The whole moral to the story is that if this widow, without any influence or power, could convince a judge to render a verdict in her favor, how much more can we come before God the righteous Judge and see Him favor us in His decisions. There are several things we learn about approaching God as Judge.

First, the Father is the Judge and rules over the judicial system of heaven and will render decisions for us from His Courts. He is an *impartial* Judge of *all* that is done on the earth.[12]

Second, we are invited to come and present our cases in the courts of Heaven. Hebrews 4:16 directs us to boldly come *"to the throne of grace, so that we may receive mercy and find grace to help in time of need."* After all, we are already seated in heavenly places at the right hand of the Father because we are in Christ Jesus (Eph. 2:6). Do you see yourself seated there? And in Isaiah 43:26, the Father, using courtroom language, directs us to present our case:

Put Me in remembrance, let us argue our case together;
State your cause, that you may be proved right [acquitted].

Putting God in remembrance as a means of presenting cases in His Courts is essential. Our Judge can only render decisions based on evidence presented. We must know how to present cases in the Courts of Heaven to get favorable verdicts.

In the story of the widow in Luke 18, when she wanted justice:

- The widow went to the courtroom and not the battlefield. The widow realized she didn't need to march onto a battlefield and yell at her adversary. She simply needed a verdict from the court.

---

[12] See Hebrews 12:23; I Pet. 1:17

- She didn't even address her adversary; she only spoke to the judge. She understood that if the Judge rendered a legal verdict, any power of the adversary would be demolished and she would win. Once this was in place her adversary had to bow the knee to the rendering of the court.

In our case, there is no need to yell, scream, or even curse our foe. All we need is a legal decision based on a verdict from Heaven and the fight is over. We can then make decrees after we revoke the enemy's legal claim in the court of Heaven.

The courts of Heaven are the place where our case against the devil is heard. In this place, the devil's claim is revoked. The courts of Heaven is for the elect and chosen of God. We don't have to fear this place but enter the Courts with great confidence by the blood of Jesus (Heb. 10:19). Romans 8:33 tells us that as the elect of God, no charge against us can stick.

> *Who will bring a charge* [in the courts of Heaven] *against God's <u>elect</u>? God is the one who justifies. (bracket and underline added)*

You are the elect or chosen of God based on Jesus' blood, the Holy Spirit's work, and God's heart toward you (1 Peter 1:1-2). You and I have status as the elect of God before His Courts. As Jesus speaks of the widow that keeps presenting her case, He declares that this is what the *elect* of God should do. The courts of Heaven are the place where we take our adversary to Court to be judged and to get a favorable verdict.

Returning to the story in Luke 18, there are several things to notice that will help us in presenting cases in the Courts of Heaven. Notice that the woman has an *adversary*. In Luke 18:3 NKJV, she was asking for judgment and justice from her adversary.

> *Now there was a widow in that city; and she came to him, saying, "Get justice for me from my <u>adversary</u>."*

The Greek word for *adversary* is *antidikos* which means "an opponent in a lawsuit." In your life and your family, you have a legal opponent that is resisting the will of God. First Peter 5:8 clearly lets us know that this *adversary* is looking for legal means to devour and destroy.

> *Be of sober spirit, be on the alert. Your adversary, the devil, prowls around like a roaring lion, seeking someone to devour.*

This word adversary in this verse is the same in the Greek that we found in Luke 18:3. It declares that we have a *legal opponent*. We are to be on guard against this legal agent, who is the devil. Otherwise, he will claim the legal right to devour and destroy the will, the desire, and intent of God in your life.

> We as the elect of God have the right to counter-sue and bring a case against our adversary.

Jesus' key take-away was this: If this widow could get a decision rendered, how much more can we as the *elect of God*. This means that the courtroom of Heaven is the place where the *elect* bring cases against our adversary. Remember that the *adversary* is the one who is attacking us with a lawsuit. However, we as the elect of God have the right to counter-sue and bring a case against our adversary. In the context of *repentance from dead works*, we repent of our efforts to earn God's acceptance and apply the blood of Christ to them before the Judge of all. Father God, the impartial Judge of all, then renders a favorable verdict for you as the elect of God! This is the *best way* to do spiritual warfare.

Jesus' Manner of Spiritual Warfare

Because you have a legal opponent or adversary, you should follow Jesus' manner of warfare against the devil. Revelation 19:11 gives us great insight into how Jesus Himself deals with His adversaries.

> *And I saw heaven opened, and behold, a white horse, and He who sat on it is called Faithful and True, and in righteousness He judges and wages war.*

Notice that Jesus has an order in which He does warfare: He *judges*, then *makes war*.

> Jesus has an order in which He does warfare: He *judges*, then *makes war.*

- *Judging* is judicial activity in a courtroom (i.e., for us, getting favorable verdicts based upon evidence – repent and apply the blood of Christ) and

- *waging war* is battlefield activity (i.e., for us, binding and loosing, declarations, decrees).

To try to make war without a favorable verdict or judgment from the court of Heaven is to suffer defeat because you have no legal footing to be on the battlefield. Anytime you challenge your adversary who claims a legal right, he will withstand you. Backlash occurs when sin-based legal claims have not been addressed in the Courts through repentance and renouncing your words and actions, which open the door for the enemy. Until the legal claims of the enemy are addressed, don't be surprised that an agitated spirit realm stirs up a reaction in the natural realm.

Once you get the legal rendering from the Father, our righteous Judge, then you can march onto the battlefield and win every time. The problem has been that we have tried to win on the battlefield without legal verdicts from Heaven backing us up. So, go into the courts of Heaven, repent and apply the blood of Jesus to cancel these sin-based legal claims against you to remove their influence and power.

> Go into the Courts of Heaven, take the blood of Jesus, and cancel these sin-based legal claims against you.

This means to first go into what the apostle Paul called the third heaven to the courts of Heaven to remove the claims against you or your family, and then go to the second heaven (where spiritual warfare is waged) and remove the enemy's influence and power (2 Cor. 12:2) using your authority to bind his efforts. To summarize, begin in the third heaven to revoke the claim and then move to the second heaven to remove the enemy. Then the Spirit of God can flow freely in your life.

We hope you have gained a better understanding of how powerful repentance is in the courts of Heaven. Make it a practice to enter the courts of Heaven to remove the legal claims of the devil and walk in the freedom Christ has provided to you.

Let's Internalize and Apply!

1. True/False: In Scripture, the place of initial victory is the courtroom and not a battlefield.

   ____

   ____

2. Where are the Courts of Heaven located?

   ____

   ____

3. True/False: You are a third-heaven creation operating in third-heaven revelation with the capacity of functioning in third-heaven authority.

4. True/False: You don't need to address your adversary in the Court of Heaven, but only speak (repent) to the Judge of all.

5. True/False: You are the elect or chosen of God based on Jesus' blood, the Holy Spirit's work, and God's heart toward you.

6. What is Jesus' order in which He does warfare?

____

____

Chapter 8

Repenting from Dead Works

In our journey to maturity, the first foundation stone we must put in place is repentance from dead works – turning away from our human efforts to please God.

The Lord wants you to have a clear conscience in His presence. He wants you to feel totally loved and accepted by Papa God with nothing standing between the two of you. However, we are often programmed by religion and at times by culture to think that we can earn the Father's love and acceptance through our human efforts, our good works, or our religious traditions. The scripture calls these efforts, *dead works*.

Dead works are efforts or works that are lifeless, that have no life in them (Gal. 3:21). They cannot justify or make us accepted before God. The scripture is very clear that none of our human efforts or traditions result in God's forgiveness and acceptance: *"There is no one who does good, not even one"* (Ps. 53:3).

> Dead works are associated with your old nature that was crucified at the Cross and left in the grave.

Regarding those who rely on their religious tradition (such as keeping the 10 Commandments or the Law), the scripture states: *"by the works of the Law no flesh is justified in His sight* (Rom. 3:20). The purpose of the Law was never to make us acceptable to God but *"to shut up everyone under sin"* (Gal. 3:22). Holding on to our human efforts to keep the Law leaves us with a *sin-consciousness* which we learned about in a previous chapter.

The Law leads *"us to Christ, so that we may be justified by faith"* (Gal. 3:24). For *"by grace you have been saved through faith; and that not of yourselves, it is the gift of God"* (Eph. 2:8). The apostle Paul described God's grace wonderfully in Titus 3:5-7:

> *He saved us, not on the basis of deeds which we have done in righteousness, but according to His mercy, by the washing of regeneration and renewing by the Holy Spirit, whom He poured out upon us richly through Jesus Christ our Savior, so that being justified by His grace we would be made heirs according to the hope of eternal life.*

Dead works are associated with your old nature that was crucified with Jesus at the cross and left in the grave. As a Christian, the Godhead only sees one version of you – the new man in Christ. Your old nature – including your dead works, human efforts, and traditions

– were nailed to the cross and do not speak on your behalf before the Father. When you adopt God's *new man* version of you, you understand that your nature and identity is righteousness --and is the basis of having a *righteousness-consciousness* view of yourself.

Unless we turn from dead works, our worship of God is in vain. God wants us to be totally dependent upon Him. When we emphasize our works, we are trying to make ourselves more acceptable and presentable to God. The only thing that makes us worthy to come into His presence is the blood of Jesus Christ.

> *Knowing that you were not redeemed with perishable things. . . but with precious blood, as of a lamb unblemished and spotless, the blood of Christ.* (I Peter 1:18-19)

Repentance is the process our loving heavenly Father has provided for you to clear the slate of dead works and obtain a clean conscience with the Father. Where does repentance occur? As we learned in the previous chapter, repentance occurs in the courts of Heaven in the unseen realm of the spirit.

Repentance in the Courtroom

Hebrews 12:24 records that the shed blood of Christ *"speaks better things"* about you before the Judge of all. Jesus brought His own blood into the holy place in heaven to speak on your behalf (Heb. 9:12). The blood of Jesus answers every accusation against you and your bloodline. Jesus' blood cries for mercy, redemption, and forgiveness for you. As a result of the testimony of the blood of Jesus on your behalf, God now has the legal right He needed to forgive you. His heart has always desired to forgive but He needed the legal right to do so. You simply need to repent of your sins (of dead works) and agree with the testimony of Jesus' blood, and receive His forgiveness because of what the blood is speaking.

It's by faith that you apply the blood of the Lord Jesus Christ. In that the blood speaks, it is declaring and gives judicial testimony on your behalf. Jesus' blood silences every voice that would dare to speak against you. It's in the heavenly courtroom where you remind the Judge of the finished work of Christ on your behalf. The death, burial, resurrection, and ascension of Christ was the legal transaction that enables the Father to forgive you of your sins.

When we know how to present this evidence in the courts of Heaven, we get the full benefit of all Jesus has done for us. We can say, "Let it be known or recorded in the courts of Heaven that the blood of Christ speaks of better things about me" (Mal. 3:16).

Here is a model prayer to help you understand and reinforce the context of repentance in the courts of Heaven in the spiritual realm:

> Lord, I come to stand before Your Courts and I want to remind You that Jesus' blood is speaking on my behalf. I thank You for the forgiveness that is mine as a result of what His blood says about me. I repent of any and every sin of dead works and ask for Jesus' blood to speak and testify for me. Thank you, Father, that Your heart is always looking to forgive. The blood of Jesus grants You the legal right You needed. I ask for the blood of Jesus to speak for me before Your Courts. I agree with what the blood is saying about me. I ask the Court to render a decision based on the testimony of His blood on my behalf. I ask, therefore, that every accusation against me because of my sins would now be forgiven and removed. Thank You Father so much for Your forgiveness and redemption. Amen.

Your part is to repent – confess as sin --the wrong thinking about acceptance in the eyes of your Father. God's part then is to forgive you. As a result, you gain a clear conscience before God. The Father deeply desires for you to have a good conscience before Him and live dependent upon Him. The Christian life, by design, is meant to be a life of dependency. You are never going to please God by living independent from Him. Genuine repentance brings in the presence of God.

Repentance means "to change one's mind." Repentance is a sincere turning away from wrong thinking. Changing your mind away from wrong thinking is the first step. The second step is to live with a new way of thinking that aligns with God's ways, will, and Word. For repentance to have its full work, there must be a *turning from* your dead works and a *turning to* Christ.

Agreeing with Our Adversary

Humility and surrender carry great weight in the courts of Heaven. Through repentance you set in place the voice of the blood of Jesus. When you sense your adversary bringing accusations against you, you should simply agree with them. This is so opposite of what your mind tells you to do. Why? Because you want to justify yourself. But Jesus says we are to agree with our adversary quickly.

Agree with your adversary quickly, while you are on the way with him, lest your adversary deliver you to the judge, the judge hand you over to the officer, and you be thrown into prison. (Matthew 5:25 NKJV).

To quickly agree with your adversary simply means that you are quick to repent of anything being used against you in the Courts. Lon speaking: My approach is I have no need to justify myself; I allow the blood of Jesus to justify and speak for me. My attitude is that I can never go wrong with repentance. Self-justification can destroy me, but repentance will cause me to be accepted. As I repent of anything in my history or even bloodline issues, the Lord will grant me repentance (2 Tim. 2:25). This takes away the accusations of the devil and silences his ability to disqualify me. If I want to have an audience in the courts, I must appear there with a humble spirit and a contrite heart (Ps. 51:17).

The End-Goal: A Clear Conscience

Repentance leads to forgiveness that results in a clear conscience, the goal the Lord has had all along. There are two types of wrong thinking that hinder us from living with a clear conscience. You have just been introduced to the first way: *having a conscience distorted by dead works.* (We will learn of the second hinderance, *having an evil conscience*, in an upcoming chapter).

Dead works is the erroneous notion that God accepts you based on your performance (*My Doing*), rather than what Jesus has done with your sins (*His Doing*).[13] Hebrews 9:14 tells us:

. . .how much more will the blood of Christ . . . cleanse your conscience from dead works to serve the living God? (Hebrews 9:14, underline added)

When you received Christ as your Savior, your spirit was cleansed of its sin nature, but you may not have purged your conscience with the truth about what Jesus has done with your sins. Satan will drag up things you have done or said to convince you that God no longer accepts you and you must *do* something to be accepted once again. Don't allow your own negative self-talk or the devil's condemnation to destroy your faith and confidence in God's acceptance. This wrong thinking will lead you to believe you don't deserve His forgiveness and favor.

---

[13] You may want to review Chapter 4 His Doing vs My Doing if you want to refresh your understanding of this truth.

Reject the lie that your acceptance by God is based on what you do and *embrace* the truth that He accepts you based 100% on Jesus' finished work. Repent and apply the cleansing blood of Christ to all of your sins and works in order to gain and live in the Father's acceptance.

Let's Discuss!

When you sin, do you ever feel condemned? How should you respond?

What does it mean to have a "righteousness-consciousness?"

Let's Internalize and Apply!

1. What are dead works?

   ____

   ____

2. How do you cleanse your conscience of "dead works?"

   ____

   ____

Chapter 9

The Completeness of Forgiveness

One of the most important understandings about your born-again spirit is:

> "I am completely forgiven of all my sins – past, present, and future."

From our experience in ministry, this truth is one of the most difficult for many Christians to understand and accept as true. You, too, may find it hard to believe and accept that the "war" between you and God regarding your sins is over and God is not mad at you. We have found that once believers understand, believe, and accept this pivotal truth of complete forgiveness, so many other truths are much easier to believe and activate. Therefore, this chapter is devoted to the subject of your complete forgiveness.

So let's look into God's spiritual mirror of the Scriptures at six aspects about your complete forgiveness. This chapter is a somewhat heavy chapter to read, but it is essential that you understand complete forgiveness in order to move forward.

First, God has forever settled the sin issue. God is not crediting or applying sin against anyone. God has not credited sin to anyone for nearly 2,000 years. The sins of the entire world have been paid for but you only benefit from this if you repent when you do sin.

I John 2:1-2 states:

> *. . . and if anyone sins, we have an Advocate with the Father, Jesus Christ the righteous; and He Himself is the propitiation for our sins; and not for ours only, but also for those of the whole world.*

Not only are your sins as a Christian forgiven and paid for, the sins of the lost have been paid for as well. Jesus bore the sins of everyone – not just those He knew would accept Him. People aren't really going to hell because of sin. They're going to hell because they have rejected Jesus' payment for their sins.

If you think God is angry with you and is holding your sins against you, then you'll never have boldness, confidence, or faith. The truth of the matter is God is not angry with you about anything once you are born again.

Jesus—who knew no sin, did no sin, and in Him was no sin -- bore the condemnation of every sin ever committed. When Jesus ascended from the grave to sit at the right hand of the Father, there was no sin upon Him because He paid the penalty for all sin at the Cross. There is no sin upon us, either, because we are in Him. Your sins were left in the grave, because they did not make it through the resurrection.

You don't want to sin. But when you do, you are not condemned (I John 2:1 above) since your sins have already been judged and condemned at the Cross. When you sin, the Holy Spirit will convict you (not condemn you) to draw you back into unity with the Lord. Let us not grieve the Holy Spirit by failing to repent of a sin.

God does not hold a sin against you that Jesus has already paid for.

God does not hold a sin against you that Jesus has already paid for. If He did, God would be putting us in double jeopardy for a sin that Jesus already paid for.

Second, you are forgiven of all sin – past, present, and future. God has forgiven you of all your sin, even sins you have not committed yet. God is no longer angry because you sin! Your forgiveness has been provided for and you *apply* that forgiveness when you confess a sin or failure.

> *. . .but through His own blood, He entered the holy place once for all, having obtained <u>eternal</u> redemption. . . those who have been called may receive the promise of the eternal inheritance.* (Hebrews 9:12c, 15, underline added)

> *. . .we have been sanctified* [positionally] *through the offering of the body of Jesus Christ once for all. . . For by one offering He has perfected for all time those who are sanctified* [process]. (Hebrews 10:10, 14, brackets added)

> *. . . and to the spirits of the righteous made perfect.* (Hebrews 12:23)

These verses show that you are forgiven of all past, present, and future sins *as you appropriate* this truth. God remembers *covenant*. The devil remembers *sin*. You get to choose which one you agree with.

Let's Discuss!

What makes it difficult for you to see yourself as your Heavenly Father sees you – as righteous, holy, perfect and complete as you will ever be? Explain.

Do you find it hard to accept the truth that the sins you have committed are already forgiven?

When Jesus died on the cross for your sins, how many of them were in the future at that time?

Third, since you are born again, sin will never be an issue between you and God.

Question: Does this mean that you can just go live in sin?

Absolutely not! How shall you being dead in your relationship to sin return to revive the power of sin in your life? This would be returning to bondage. As a new creation, you have been set free of the power of sin! You do not want to go back and live in sin. Why?

Sin enslaves.

> *. . .when you present yourselves to someone as slaves for obedience, you are slaves of the one whom you obey, either of sin resulting in death, or of obedience resulting in righteousness?* Romans 6:16

> *Stand fast therefore in the liberty by which Christ has made us free, and do not be entangled again with a yoke of bondage.* Galatians 5:1 NKJV

Even though you are in Christ, the flesh remains dormant within you. In your born-again spirit, you are dead in your relationship to sin, so do not return to sin and revive it again! If you revive the flesh, you resurrect it and it is no longer dormant. The "beast" in you is sleeping, it's not dead. Choose to not walk according to the flesh (our old nature) but walk according to the Spirit (in our born-again spirit).

> *Even so consider yourselves to be dead to sin, but alive to God in Christ Jesus. (*Romans 6:11)

Consider yourself dead to sin. The Father does.

> In your spirit, you are dead in your relationship to sin, so do not return to sin and revive it again!

You do not have to sin. To do so is to allow sin to "reign" in your mortal body. If you do, you certainly will not lose your salvation, but you will suffer the consequences of choosing to live *independent* of God. Do not get entangled again with a yoke (or attachment) to sin. If you sin, "crucify the flesh with its passions and desires" (Gal. 5:24). Put it to death by repenting and applying the blood of Christ to it! Your born-again spirit desires purity and liberty, that which is holy and righteous, so follow your spirit.

> *Having these promises, beloved, let us cleanse ourselves from all defilement of flesh and spirit, perfecting holiness in the fear of God. (*2 Corinthians 7:1)

Sinning violates the unity you have with the Lord and your spiritual oneness with Him.

You have the responsibility to safeguard your body from sin and keep it from being used as an instrument of unrighteousness. Failing to do so would be to *violate the unity* you have with the Lord and your spiritual oneness with Him. Sinning against your own body involves sinning against the Jesus to whom you are united, allowing sin to reign in your mortal body.

> *. . .consider yourselves to be dead to sin, but alive to God in Christ Jesus. Therefore do not let sin reign in your mortal body so that you obey its lusts.* (Romans 6:11-12)

In Christ, your relationship to sin has died. But when you give in to the temptation to sin as a Christian, you are once again giving sin power in your life by resurrecting it. The power of the flesh (soul + body) is strong and alluring, but when it makes its appeal, you don't have to respond. Choose to firmly resist temptation and preserve the unity you have with Jesus!

Sin gives an inroad for Satan to work in your life.

If you go out and live in sin, you're inviting Satan in. You're opening a door for the devil to work in your life.

Sinning is foolish. If you choose to live in sin, you're not smart. But God loves you. God is not holding your sin against you, but you are inviting the devil into your life. You are not going to prosper if you choose to live in sin. You will hinder, handicap, and even nullify the grace of God because you are not cooperating with God. You are called to freedom, so stay free!

> *For you were called to freedom, brethren; only do not turn your freedom into an opportunity for the flesh, but through love serve one another.* (Galatians 5:13)

Sin, whether in word or action, results in a bad harvest.

There is an overriding principle in scripture that every seed sown will result in a harvest. While the earth remains, there will always be seedtime and harvest. With our words, we either speak words of life or words of death. Words and actions of life and death have been set before us, resulting in a harvest of blessing or of death. We are commanded to choose life with our words and our actions. Jesus tells us that seedtime and harvest is how the kingdom of God works. There will always be a harvest. (Gen. 8:22; Prov. 18:21; Deut. 30:19; Mark 4:26-29).

Take a few minutes now and ask Holy Spirit to examine your heart to identity any negative seeds you have sown with your words or your actions. You only want a good harvest and not a bad one. Pray this prayer to cancel negative words and actions:

> "Lord, forgive me for every harmful word I have spoken against myself or others, and in the mighty name of Jesus Christ, I take authority over and cancel and break the power of every harmful or negative word I have spoken about me or others. Any assignment the enemy has put in motion by such words, let it be cancelled and nullified now in Jesus' name.
>
> In the mighty name of Jesus Christ, I break off any assignment, plot, and scheme by the enemy that my words have opened doors to and cancel their effect over my life, my family, even the nation. I command any doors opened through my actions be legally closed now in the name of Jesus Christ. Let no word curse, or negative words spoken by me take root in my life and bear harmful fruit. Let it be uprooted now in Jesus' name.
>
> I speak life and life more abundant and blessing over my life, my family's life, over others, and the nation in Jesus' name. In the name of Jesus Christ, Lord, order my words, let them be released in authority, in power, in wisdom, and be pleasing and acceptable to You, in Jesus' name."

Fourth, God does not impute (hold) sin against you and will not hold future sin against you.

> *. . .just as David also speaks of the blessing on the man to whom God credits* [imputes] *righteousness apart from works: Blessed are those whose lawless deeds have been forgiven* [past tense], *and whose sins have been covered* [past tense]; *Blessed is the man whose sin the Lord will not* [future tense] *take into account* [impute sin]." (Romans 4:6-8, brackets added)

Your actions or wrong thinking do not define your identity in Christ.

This verse says God "will not" impute (credit) *sin* to you, because He has already imputed *righteousness* to you. Everything is a legal matter in the courts of Heaven when it comes to Heaven and the spirit realm. When you were born again, all of your sins – past, present, and even future sins – were laid on Jesus. God will never in the future hold sins against you! When you do sin, it is your responsibility to confess that sin and thank God that this sin has already been forgiven. In so doing, you are not letting sin negatively affect your heart, your body, and your relationships.

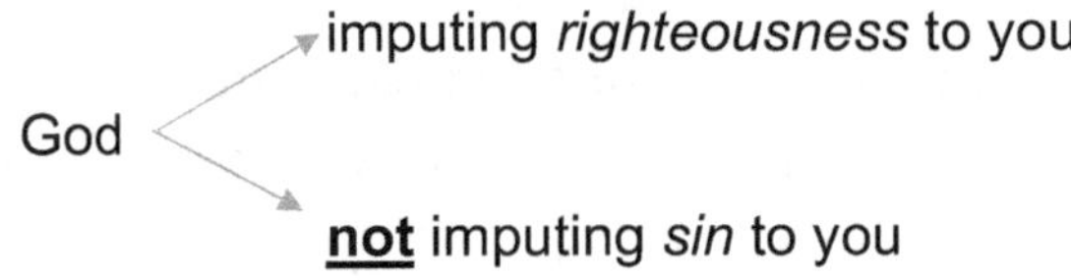

Christ's finished work is not benefiting you if you fall into religious thinking that says,

> "I've been saved by grace, but now that I am a Christian, I need to pray, fast, tithe, study, and attend church in order for God to love me, bless me, use me, and answer my prayers."

You know that God is powerful, but you may think, "How could He ever use His power on my behalf?" This puts you back under a sin-consciousness rather than a righteous-consciousness, thinking you have to perform to keep God's favor. You begin to doubt God's willingness to use His ability on your behalf because you feel He is still holding sin against you.

This is religion speaking and not the Bible. Religion puts the focus on what *you* need to do instead of what *Christ* has already done. Religion is all about your "doing" – that's behavior modification.

Your acceptance is found at the Cross because the Father was fully satisfied with Jesus' payment for your sins. Now, your heavenly Father assesses you based on what Jesus has already done. When you do sin, repent and thank Him that this sin is forgiven. Remember, to the extent that God the Father is *satisfied* with Jesus' finished work, He is *satisfied with you*!

In summary, God placed all your sin upon Jesus. All your sin. Sin is a non-issue with God. He is aware of when you sin and will strongly impress upon you to quit doing it, but not because He's going to reject you. He's already paid for it. God is not ignorant of sin in your life, but it does not change His attitude toward you. Holy Spirit will point to that sin in your life as a place of your next upgrade in your relationship with the Father. Jesus paid for your sin – past, present, and even future sins. When God looks at you, He sees your born-again spirit – which is as eternally righteous and holy as Jesus!

What you may have done (sin, failure) is *not* who you are. Your actions or wrong thinking do not define your identity in Christ. What God has said about you, and provided through Jesus Christ, defines your identity.

Let's Discuss!

Do you feel that God is imputing or holding a sin against you? If so, are you thinking with a 'sin consciousness' or with a 'righteousness consciousness?'

How can you flip the script to see God imputing righteousness to you?

Fifth, God does not put a timeline on your forgiveness!

Every time you sin, the Lord doesn't have to wait until you repent in order to get that sin under the Blood and then be forgiven. Our redemption in Christ was not a short-term redemption – that is, only good until the next time you sin (and then have to repent, get the Blood reapplied, and be forgiven again).

The truth is Christ entered the holy place once and obtained for us an *eternal* redemption. God's grace is *cheapened* when you think He has only forgiven you of your sins up to the point you are saved, and after that point, you must depend on your confession of sins to be forgiven. God's forgiveness is not given in *installments*.

If you believe God's forgiveness is given in installments, you won't be able to expect God to protect, provide, and prosper you. It will rob you of your ability to receive God's goodness, blessings, unmerited favor, and success.

God's forgiveness is not given in *installments*.

Lon speaking: *This truth about no timeline on forgiveness was very difficult for me to accept for a number of years. I felt that my sins were forgiven up to a point – up to the most recent time that I confessed my sins – but not since that time. I felt He was still holding these latter sins against me. This is what religion had taught me, and not the Bible. Religion had put the focus on what I needed to do instead of what Christ has already done.*

I was living with a sin consciousness with a pretty strong emotional attachment to that wrong understanding. I was listening to the wrong voice (religion) rather than God's voice that says I am completely forgiven of all my sins – past, present, and future. Now, I have the Spirit's revelation of the completeness of God's forgiveness. I am free to live with a righteousness consciousness in my born-again spirit; I am completely forgiven!

So now when I sin, I quickly repent of it out of my love for the Lord and thank Him that this sin was forgiven on the Cross two-thousand years ago. I rejoice that my loving heavenly Father forgave me of all my sins and I appropriate that forgiveness when I repent!

Let's Discuss!

Do you put a timeline on God's forgiveness of your sins?

Do you feel that God has only forgiven you up to a point in time?

Moving forward, how can you regularly appropriate God's forgiveness on an on-going basis?

Sixth, God has completely qualified you in your standing before Him! He has qualified you for all His blessings through the shed blood of Jesus Christ on the cross, and His burial and resurrection.

> *giving thanks to the Father, who has qualified us to share in the inheritance of the saints in Light.* (Colossians 1:12, underline added)

Do you ever feel unqualified for God's acceptance? We have good news! You are fully qualified to share in the full inheritance that is yours!

Don't fall into the trap of looking at your life, imperfections and failings, and start to disqualify yourself from receiving God's blessings and favor. You may be tempted to think, "Why would God bless me? Look at what I've done. I am so undeserving." Instead of having faith to believe God for breakthroughs, you may feel too condemned to believe in God's goodness and receive what He has already provided when He qualified you.

All your *disqualifications* exist in the *natural* realm. You live and operate in the *supernatural* (spiritual) realm where God has *qualified* you with His grace. God has fully qualified you in your born-again spirit. Remember, you are the righteousness of God in Christ Jesus.

Say out loud: "I am fully qualified to share in His inheritance!"

Let's summarize: Because of the finished work of Christ at Calvary, God has not credited, or imputed, sin against anyone for nearly 2,000 years. What God has imputed to you is "everlasting righteousness" (Dan. 9:24). Christ paid for all sins – past, present, and even future for every person for all time. The war is over. God is no longer angry because of your sin. Your sin is no longer an issue with God.

The war concerning your sin is over as far as heaven is concerned. This is such good news! The completeness of forgiveness is a truth that will transform you if you will receive the revelation of that forgiveness. You will view the Father in a different light -- as loving, gracious, and good.

Let's Discuss!

What are some of the ways you disqualify yourself from God's blessings?

How can you flip the script and walk in the truth that you are fully qualified in the eyes of your heavenly Father?

Let's Internalize and Apply!

1. Are the sins I commit an issue for God the Father? Why or why not?

 ____

 ____

2. When you were born again, how many of your sins were forgiven? Today, how many of your sins are forgiven? Which of your sins today are unforgiven?

 ____

 ____

3. Does God put a timeline on His forgiveness of your sins?

 ____

 ____

4. If you die as a Christian with unconfessed sin, do you go to heaven or hell?

 ____

 ____

Chapter 10

The Gift of a Good Conscience

But the goal of our instruction is love from a pure heart and a good conscience and a sincere faith. (1 Timothy 1:5)

One of the wonderful gifts that the Father has provided you through the finished work of Christ is the gift of a good conscience. In the verse above, the apostle Paul stated that having a good conscience and pure heart before God is foundational to walking in love and faith. If you don't have an accurate and upgraded conscience before God, then you will have a distorted and incomplete view of your true identity in Christ. This will interfere with your relationship with God – not feeling fully accepted by Him. You have already learned that you are totally accepted by the Father; let that truth be fully activated in your heart!

The apostles Paul and Peter declare the lack of a good conscience before God can negatively affect your relationship with others (1 Tim. 1:19; 1 Pet. 3:16). Not feeling fully accepted by the Father can open the door for feelings of rejection by others.

How do you develop a good conscience before God?

You develop a good conscience by having a scriptural understanding of two things: the completeness of your forgiveness by the Father (the previous chapter) and the gift of no condemnation.

Let's first learn about this wonderful gift of no condemnation and then what is required to have a good conscience.

God the Father has given you the *gift of no condemnation!*

> *Therefore, there is now no condemnation for those who are in Christ Jesus. . . Who is the one who condemns?* Romans 8:1, 34

God has given you the *gift of no condemnation*! The more you *believe* that you are righteous in Christ and *refuse to accept condemnation* for your past mistakes and present temptations, the more you will be set free from hindrances and addictions that bind you.

Even though you fail, there is no condemnation because you are in Christ and all your sins were washed away by His Blood. When God looks at you, He doesn't focus on your failures. God sees you as a *learner*, not a failure. As Jesus is spotless and without blame, so are you in your born-again spirit (the 'real' you)! Remember, as Jesus is now, so are you in this world (I John 4:17).

> God sees you as a *learner*, not a failure.

Make this declaration out loud:

> I am *free from condemnation* because Jesus has given me the gift of no-condemnation!

If you feel condemned, it is not from God. Your own conscience may smite you, and Satan – the accuser of the brethren – may condemn you, but God does not.

When you do something wrong, you will sense a conviction from the Holy Spirit to repent of that sin. However, the feeling of condemnation is different – it's an *assault* against your sonship in Christ. That assault is either from Satan or your conscience, but it is not from God. Conviction from the Holy Spirit leads you to repentance and draws you into closer fellowship with the Lord; condemnation leads you to despair and hopelessness.

> Condemnation is an *assault* against your sonship in Christ.

Condemnation does not come from the Godhead! Neither God the Father, nor Jesus, nor the Holy Spirit are condemning you (Romans 8:31-35). Your own heart may condemn you, and you may have blamed it on God. But God is *not* angry with you. God is not out to "get you." He is not even in a bad mood. God loves you! The Lord is truly at peace with you!

Remember, God the Father has given you the *gift of no condemnation*, which gives you the power to overcome your weaknesses and failures!

Let's look now at how to reject condemnation and develop a good conscience.

Condemnation Source #1: Our Adversary

> *No weapon that is formed against you will prosper; And every tongue that accuses you in judgment you will condemn. This is the heritage of the servants of the Lord, And their vindication* [righteousness] *is from Me, declares the Lord.* (Isaiah 54:17, bracket added)

We often quote this verse, but we should start at the end of the verse: you are declared righteous! That is an identity statement. Knowing that you are righteous in your born-again spirit enables you to confidently condemn and firmly reject every tongue of accusation, judgment, and condemnation that rises against you.

Action Step: Start speaking and maintaining your belief and confession that you are righteous. Use your faith for the most important thing -- believing that you are the righteousness of God in your spirit.

The adversary pours accusation on you using the *voice of a legalist* to disqualify you. (Because he is a legalist, you must repent, apply the blood of Christ, and declare in the courtroom of Heaven that you already have the gift of no condemnation!) He uses the voice of religion to accuse. Your adversary uses the law and commandments to show your failures, and to put a *spotlight on how your behavior has disqualified you* from fellowship with God, pointing out how undeserving you are of His acceptance, love, and blessings. He uses the law to heap condemnation upon you and give you a sense of guilt and distance from God. Your enemy knows that the more condemnation and guilt you experience, the more likely you are to feel alienated from God and continue in sin. (Remember, you are *fully qualified* to participate in His inheritance; embrace it!)

However, you should not allow the devil to condemn you for not keeping the Law; for the Law is for the unbeliever, and not for the righteous person.

> *But we know that the Law is good, if one uses it lawfully, realizing the fact that <u>law is not made for a righteous person</u>, but for those who are lawless and rebellious, for the ungodly and sinners, for the unholy and profane. . . (*I Timothy 1:8-9c)

If you will accept, believe, and rest in your identity in Christ, and live and walk in the Holy Spirit, you will supernaturally keep, and even exceed, the requirements of the Law. Focusing on the law keeps you aware of sin. But focusing on righteousness by grace develops in you a righteousness consciousness -- which is how heaven views you!

The Litmus Test

The voice of accusation and condemnation only works if your adversary can get you to focus on *your* doing rather than *His* doing.

My Doing		His Doing
Self-occupied	vs:	Christ occupied
Self-conscious	vs:	Christ conscious
Me	vs:	my identity in Christ
My doing	vs:	Christ's doing/finished work

God is no shamer or fault-finder. He is no longer angry because of your sin!

Another Action Step: *Put the spotlight on the finished work of* Christ, who on the Cross took your condemnation and qualified you to receive God's acceptance, love, and favor forever!

Receive the gift of no condemnation, as it will give you the power to overcome your weaknesses and failures!

Condemnation Source #2: A conscience not fully transformed to a 'righteousness consciousness' belief system.

The second hinderance to a good conscience is the erroneous belief that your core self (your spirit) as a Christian is still sinful in some way. You still have a *sin-consciousness* rather than a *righteousness-consciousness.* Scripture calls this wrong view an *evil conscience*. Hebrews 10:22 records:

> *. . .let us draw near with a sincere heart in full assurance of faith, having our hearts sprinkled clean from an evil conscience. . .*

If you have an evil conscience, you still think that there are two versions of you: your new nature and your old nature. God only sees one version of you – the new man (Eph. 2:15; 4:24). You need to see the real you as having a *righteousness-consciousness*, which is how the Godhead sees you. Repent of continuing to believe that you have a sin-*consciousness* and embrace the real you – a *righteousness* version of you.

You will need to reprogram your conscience. Your conscience may have been programmed with a wrong belief system (from the old self or religion) based on dead works or an evil conscience, and needs to be upgraded. Make this declaration out loud:

> "I am as *righteous* and *holy, perfect* and *complete* as Jesus.

You need to embrace a *righteousness* view of who you are! Keep believing and declaring this over time and soon you will give your conscience a much-needed upgrade!

Let's Discuss!

When you sin, do you ever feel condemned? How should you respond?

What does it mean to have a "righteousness-consciousness?"

Let's Internalize and Apply!

1. When you feel condemned, what is/are the source(s)?

   ____

   ____

2. What are dead works? How do you cleanse your conscience of "dead works?"

   ____

   ____

3. What is meant by an "evil conscience?" What is the remedy for an evil conscience?

   ____

   ____

4. Will your born-again spirit be further "cleansed" when you get to heaven?

   ____

   ____

Chapter 11

"Give Me Back My Stuff!"

(An Application Process)

"Let us lay aside [renounce] *every weight,* [wrong perception] *and the sin which so easily ensnares us. (*Heb. 12:1 NKJV, brackets added)

We have grown up in a world that is pretty negative. The world is inherently negative but the Kingdom isn't. Negatives are those things which are not a part of your new nature in Christ or the fruit of the Spirit. Negative thoughts and feelings manifest in such behaviors as anxiety and worry, fear, anger, doubt and unbelief, and frustration. There are no negative thoughts and feelings in heaven so we should not allow them in our mind or heart.

> All negativity wars against your identity in Christ, against your sonship in Christ.

Negatives are a wrong perception about who you are. They are not how heaven perceives or views you. All negativity wars against your identity in Christ, against your sonship in Christ. Your biggest battles are always about your true identity.

Negativity and negative self-talk do not belong to you; they are not a part of your new man in Christ. Jesus paid dearly for them, therefore, they don't belong to you. They belong to Jesus, so put off these things and give them back to Jesus. He crucified and buried them for you, and He did not bring them through the resurrection. He only resurrected your new self in newness of life. Consider yourself dead to these negative things and remove them from your soul.

How do you get rid of negatives? First, you remove negatives by repenting of them. Be careful of the agreements that you make and speak. Second, invite Holy Spirit to help you keep your mind and heart in perfect peace by keeping your mind on the one true version of you – your new man.

> Your biggest battles are always about your true identity.

The Duck and the Sponge

We each respond to negativity in different ways in differing situations. But we seem to have a propensity to respond in one of two ways.

You may be a person who tends to be a **sponge** as you respond to negativity. For example, someone may say something negative about you. As a sponge soaks up water, you respond by absorbing the negative thought and negative feeling associated with the negative comment. If you don't squeeze out that negative thought and feeling, you begin to adopt it as a part of your identity and act accordingly.

Or, you may be a person who generally responds to negativity like a **duck**. You don't seem to let negative thoughts bother you, as you let the thought and feeling associated with the negative comment run off "like water off of a duck's back."

Laurie speaking: *I have a melancholy temperament so I tend to absorb feelings of negativity like a sponge pretty easily. When I hear a negative statement made, I often absorb the feeling and the thinking that goes with it. Lon not so much, as he tends to respond to negativity like a duck. He doesn't seem to let negative thoughts bother him very much as he typically will not accept those words or feelings.*

Let's Discuss!

When it comes to responding to negativity, do you tend to respond like a sponge or like a duck?

Jesus Said, "Give Me Back My Stuff!"

We want to share a dream that Graham Cook shared about being caught up to heaven.[14]

Graham said that he had similar dreams as this one where Jesus was marching up a grassy hill with a smile on His face and was hugging others along the way. This time, Jesus was marching up the hill to him looking annoyed.

Jesus: *"Give me back my stuff!"*

Graham: "I don't know what you mean, Lord."

Jesus: *"Graham, don't mess with me. Give me back my stuff!"*

Graham: "I don't know what you mean."

Jesus: *"Sure you do. Give me back my stuff! I want it. And I want it right now!"*

Graham: "Jesus, I gave you everything. Honest."

---

[14] Graham Cooke, Jesus Demanded Graham Cooke, "Give Me Back My Stuff," https://www.youtube.com/watch?v=A-dBioGxk0E, July 7, 2014

Jesus: *"You took some stuff from me and I don't want you to have it. Now give it back to me."*

Graham: "I really don't know what you mean Lord."

Jesus: *"This is the last time. Give me back my stuff."*

Graham: "What stuff?"

Jesus: *"All that worry, that anger, that resentment, bitterness, fear. I died for it. I paid a price for it. It belongs to me. It doesn't belong to you. Give me back my stuff!"*

Graham: "Oh my God, I now get it. All those things You died for, You took them to the cross, and I've been resurrecting them. And I'm utterly appalled. I'm so sorry."

Jesus: *"Do you have any idea how delighted I was to die for all those things? When I was on the cross, it was the joy that was set before Me to die for all those things. On the cross, I knew that I was robbing you of experiencing all that negativity. I was taking all those things so that you would never have to experience them ever again. I can give you a whole new life where all those things are absent."*

"Do you know how excited I was to take all those things away from you – to never be fearful again, or worried or panicked? To never have to be angry, or bitter or resentful? To never have to do any of that stuff again? You can be free of all negativity."

"All your negative ways of looking at things that make you cynical and sarcastic. All your negative ways of seeing or thinking. Ways that make you imagine the worst before seeing the best."

"I robbed you of all that negativity so you can <u>see</u> the best, <u>think</u> the best, <u>believe</u> the best, and <u>be</u> the best."

"And you keep taking it all back, like it belongs to you. It doesn't belong to you. I died for it. I paid a price for it. It's mine. Give Me back my stuff. You can't have it."

"All the time you are taking hold of these things, you can't see who you really are in Me. You can't be the person I see when I look at you. Every time you take up all those things, there is a disconnect between you and heaven. I died so that you could stay connected with heaven. It's called, abiding – staying, remaining in that place in Me." Then you can have My accelerated goodness, My grace, My power."

My son, I want my stuff back. You and I have important things to do."

End of dream.

When Graham awoke from the dream, he said he wrote down all the things he had taken from Jesus. Next to those things he wrote all the positive things that were the opposite of those negative things. He turned each negative into a positive and began living from his true identity in Christ and manifesting the fruit of the Spirit.

Let's Discuss!

What things have you taken from Jesus that He died for?

What do you need to repent of and give back to Him?

How can you replace those things with the fruit of the Spirit in your life?

Making War on Negativity

Negativity is not a part of your identity in Christ.

Every negative, whether anxiety, worry, fear, doubt, or frustration, becomes a weight that hinders the free manifestation of your true identity in Christ (Heb. 12:1).

You are to lay aside every weight, all negativity which so easily entangles you. They don't belong to you. They are not a part of your true identity in Christ.

- All negativity is an assault against your identity in Christ.
- Negatives distract you from your true identity and destiny.
- Negatives can distort how you perceive who you really are in Christ.
- Negatives challenge the truths God has declared about you.

> All negativity is an assault against your identity in Christ.

You may know from experience that negativity leads to wrong perceptions about God and about yourself, and manifests as negative behavior, negative thinking, negative emotions, sarcasm, and cynicism. However, the Holy Spirit wants to expose the lies of negativity about your true identity and wants to correct how you *see* yourself, *think* about yourself, and *talk* about yourself.

All of your negatives have already been addressed at the Cross.

Here's the good news! All negatives were crucified and buried in Christ with our sins. Negativity is a part of the old man, not the new man.

The shed blood of Christ has already paid for all negatives in your life. They don't belong to you. Our perspective needs to be:

> If it doesn't exist in heaven, it can't exist here.
>
> If it is not in Christ, you don't want it. Don't accept it.

A negative is a weight that was crucified and buried in Christ along with your sins. Let your sin and all negativity, buried with Christ, remain in the grave.

When you are weary and heavy-laden -- with all your negative attachments, negative thinking, negative emotions -- Jesus directs you to come to Him and give Him your negatives. He will give you rest. He invites you to take His yoke and learn from Him (Matt. 11:28-30). When you do, His yoke is easy and light because there are no negatives attached to it. Consider yourself dead to all negativity and give it back to Jesus. His yoke does not contain any negativity.

Negativity presses against your born-again spirit and your walk in the Spirit.

Negatives press against your walk in the Spirit and the full expression of the fruit of the Spirit. The lies of all negatives press against and challenge:

- your *perception* of what's true in your born-again spirit, (which is as righteous, complete, and perfect as Jesus is now)
- how you *think* and *feel* about yourself, and
- how you *talk* about yourself.

Negatives will seek to restrict, frustrate, or even nullify the flow of God's grace in your life (Gal. 2:21). Since you are crucified with Christ, and your old nature is in the grave, don't let negativity arise to frustrate the flow of the grace of God in your life.

Think of a negative as a way of life that is taught by the flesh, the world and religion. A negative can become a behavior pattern, a way of thinking or feeling that is unhelpful. A negative is a thought or feeling you have *given consent to* that can never produce His fullness of life in you. You now have a consensual relationship with that negative and you must come out of agreement with it.

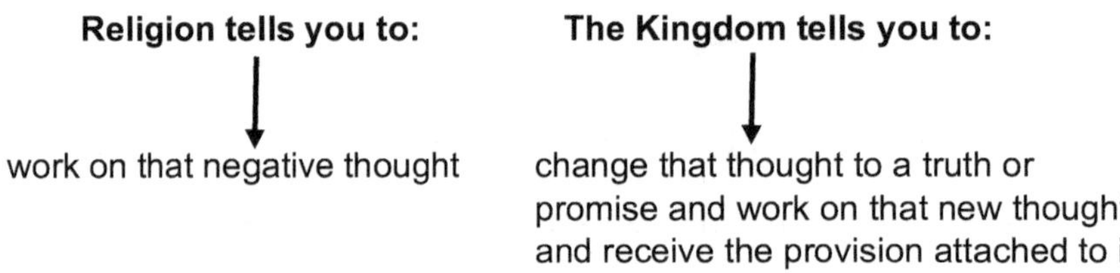

For example, religion tells you to work on your negative thought, say worry. On the other hand, the Kingdom tells you not to think about worry, but to change it into a promise such as, "cast all your anxieties on Him, because He cares for you" (1 Pet. 5:7). Work on that instead and receive God's provision of rest attached to it. Give Jesus back your worries – about life, about tomorrow, about what you eat, drink, or wear. These worries don't belong to you.

The Kingdom never works on a negative (using behavior modification); rather, Holy Spirit works *within* you by prompting you to change that negative thought into a truth about your identity, and He works on that thought. Holy Spirit seeks to convert the negative or wrong perception into something that is true about the new man so He can deal with it. The Godhead only works on your new man, never the old. God only speaks to you from your identity in Christ. The Lord refuses to work with a negative because there are no negatives in heaven.

Let's do what 1 Peter 5:7 instructs us to do, *"casting all your anxiety on Him, because He cares for you."* The word "anxiety" in the Greek is *merimna,* which means "to divide and fracture a person's being into parts." Anxiety (cares, worries) draws you away from the main thing, which is to be single minded about who you are in Christ. If you become mentally preoccupied on the negatives, you will lock in and become double-minded – a person of two minds (James 1:8). The scripture records, *"I hate those who are double-*

minded" (Ps. 119:113). So, give Jesus back His stuff – all the negatives in its various forms – and walk single-focused on your new man in Christ!

Application Steps

Follow these four steps to give your negatives back to Jesus:

STEP 1: Identity all the negatives that you are holding onto that are not a part of your new nature in Christ. They may be negative thoughts, feelings, and behavior. Examples: anxieties, worries, doubts and unbelief, fears, frustrations, sarcasm, or cynicism.

STEP 2: In prayer, give each negative thought/feeling/behavior back to Jesus. Remember, negatives are part of the old nature that do not belong to you. You must *come out of consensual agreement* with each negative. Jesus will give you rest, so accept His invitation to take His yoke and learn from Him because His yoke does not contain any negativity.

STEP 3: For each negative, identify an opposite positive that God has declared about you in His Word. These positives will include truths, identity statements, or fruit of the Spirit that are a part of your new man. Consider yourself dead to all negativity and give it back to Jesus.

STEP 4: Declare/confess each positive daily or several times each day, especially when you discern a negative is trying to re-surface in your life.

Let's Internalize and Apply!

1. T/F All negativity is at war against your identity or sonship in Christ.

2. Are negativity and negative self-talk a part of your new man in Christ?

   ____

   ____

3. When Jesus says to give Him back His stuff, what does He want returned?

   ____

   ____

4. In what four ways does negativity war against your true identity in Christ?

____

____

5. In what three areas does negativity press against your born-again spirit?

____

____

6. Negativity can be thought of as an attachment or weight to your life that comes from what three sources?

____

____

7. What does the kingdom of God tell you to focus on regarding a negative thought? How does this differ from what religion tells you to do?

____

____

8. T/F The Lord refuses to work with a negative because there are no negatives in heaven.

Section 4

The *Faith in God* Principle

As you learned in the previous section, the outcome from repenting of dead works -- your efforts to gain the Father's love and acceptance – is to gain a clear conscience before God. You have repented of your efforts and called upon the blood of Christ to cleanse you in the courts of Heaven.

We now move on to the next principle – *faith toward God.* The outcome of the *faith in God* principle is that you graduate from having a sin-consciousness view of yourself, and embrace a *righteousness consciousness* view of yourself. After all, this is the version that Father God has of you as the new man in Christ.

In Chapter 12, you will learn what it means to have faith in God. In Chapter 13, you will learn the importance of developing a righteousness view of yourself. Finally, in Chapter 14, you will learn a practical process to remove the sin-consciousness view and replace it with the desired view of righteous-consciousness.

Chapter 12

Faith in God

We come now to the second principle: *faith in God*. This second principle is intertwined with the first principle of *repentance from dead works* in the context of the courts of Heaven. Think of these first two principles as two complementary sides of a coin.

Let's recap who and what speaks for you in the courts of Heaven. First, the Father, who is the Judge of all, is on your side. How do you know? He delivered up his Son for you (Rom. 8:31-32)! Second, Jesus is for you. He died for you and shed His blood for you. Jesus is now at the right hand of the Father always interceding for you as your advocate and defense attorney.[15] You have the best lawyer and Advocate – Jesus! And better yet, His Father is the Judge. The odds are in your favor with this Judge and your defense attorney.

Furthermore, Jesus' shed blood *"speaks better things"* about you in the courts of Heaven before the Judge of all (Heb. 12:24). The blood of Jesus answers every accusation against you, cleansing your conscience of dead works and an evil conscience (removing the old version of you so you can focus exclusively on your new nature). With both the Father and Jesus rooting for you, you cannot lose!

As you learned in the previous section, scripture uses courtroom language to describe the receiving of salvation. Repentance from dead works occurs in the spirit realm in the court of Heaven, resulting in your forgiveness. Your belief and acceptance of the finished work of Christ (death, burial, resurrection, and seating in heaven) for your salvation is also recognized in the courts of Heaven. This expression of your faith in God is referred to as the *doctrine of justification*.

The Two-fold Work of Christ

Understanding the doctrine of justification includes three biblical or theological terms: redemption, propitiation, and justification. The doctrine of justification is often represented as a triangle, called The Salvation Triangle.

---

[15] Romans 8:34; Hebrews 7:25

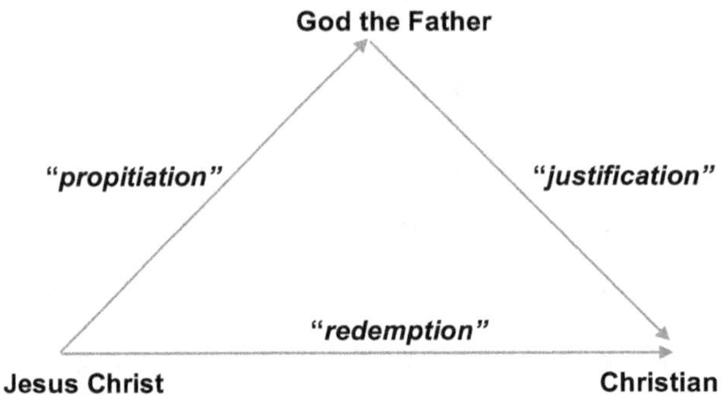

Notice that God justifies you based on the two-fold work of Christ. First, along the bottom of the triangle, Christ rescued you from sin by *redeeming* you: *"you were redeemed with. . . the precious blood of Christ* (I Pet. 1:18-19). Jesus redeemed you by purchasing you with His own blood. This is what *He did* for you, not what you *could do* for yourself.

Second, along the left side of the triangle, Jesus satisfied the Father's righteous anger, wrath, and fiery indignation against all of your sins.[16] He turned aside the Father's wrath forever (known as *propitiation*) through His sacrificial death. This is what Jesus did for you in relation to the Father. The apostle John writes of this work of Christ:

> *If anyone sins, we have an Advocate with the Father, Jesus Christ the righteous; and He Himself is the propitiation for our sins; and not for ours only, but also for those of the whole world.* (I John 2:1b – 2).

God the Father was fully satisfied with the payment of His Son on the cross and will never be angry with you about your sin. When it was completed, Jesus shouted, "It is finished!" Jesus permanently turned aside God's wrath, anger, and fury against your sin through his sacrifice of atonement.

So Jesus made a double payment – *redemption* and *propitiation* -- for all sins for all time, taking the full brunt of the punishment you deserved, satisfying God's justice (Is. 40:2). The apostle Paul wrote that the finished work of Christ made us *"one new man"* when He reconciled us to the Father (Eph. 2:15-16). Now, God is in total peace with you because the full payment for your sin was completed nearly 2000 years ago!

Lon speaking: *I've always understood that Jesus redeemed me as a result of His work on the Cross, but I did not understand His propitiatory work. When I committed a sin, I*

[16] See Isaiah 53:10-11; 54:9-10

wrongly thought that if I did not quickly repent, God would be angry with me. As a result, I was not fully trusting the Father since I was sure that "the other shoe was going to drop" on me because of a sin for which I had not repented. I did not understand that Jesus took the full brunt of the Father's anger toward my sin and now if I do sin, it does not separate me from the Lord. Now I know God is in total peace with me. The war is over!

The good news is that on the basis of Christ's *redemptive* and *propitiatory* work, God is right in *justifying* you (along the right side of the triangle). In the courts of Heaven, you now can freely remind the Judge that the shed blood of Christ speaks better things of you. All of your sins – past, present, and future - have been fully paid!

God's *holiness* is now on your side. His *righteousness* is now for you, not against you. You are His beloved in whom He is well pleased because of Jesus' finished work. He is delighted with you.

Summary of Justification

Justification, then, is heaven's decision *for* you that is rendered by the *"Judge of all,"* based on the two-fold work of Christ of redemption and propitiation. Picture the Father's verdict where He justifies you in the courts of Heaven. Jesus took all of the guilt and punishment that you should have received and He gave to you His righteousness instead. The scriptural foundation for the doctrine of justification transpiring in the courts of Heaven is captured in these verses:

> *Therefore, having been <u>justified by faith</u>, we have peace with God through our Lord Jesus Christ, through whom also we have obtained our introduction by faith into this grace in which we stand.* (Romans 5:1-2)
>
> *For by grace you have been <u>saved through faith</u>; and that not of yourselves, it is the gift of God; not as a result of works, so that no one may boast.* (Ephesians 2:8-9)

How do you obtain and walk in justification?

First, repent of your dead works as a way to gain God's acceptance. Forsake this approach so you can walk in a position of justification before God (the *Repentance from Dead Works* Principle).

If we confess our sins, He is faithful and righteous to forgive us our sins and to cleanse of from all righteousness. (I John 1:9)

Second, accept Jesus Christ as your satisfactory payment for sin through faith in His blood and gain the status of justified (the *Faith in God* Principle). Romans 3:24 – 25 summarizes the entire doctrine of justification when it states:

Being justified as a gift by His grace through redemption which is in Christ Jesus; whom God displayed publicly as a propitiation in His blood through faith. (Romans 3:24-25)

Finally, believe that God has accepted your repentance and faith in Christ Jesus, making you His child. *For you are all sons of God through faith in Christ Jesus"* (Gal. 3:26).

The ultimate goal of fully accepting and implementing the *faith in God* principle is for you to adopt a *righteousness* view of yourself. You stop seeing yourself as a sinner (with a sin consciousness) but rightly see yourself as a righteous saint. A *saint* is one who is recognized as holy through the blood of Christ in the courts of Heaven. You can honestly and genuinely say:

"I no longer see myself as a sinner, but as a saint. . . who occasionally sins."

Yes, you will occasionally sin, and when you do, Holy Spirit will convict you. You will sense this in your conscience. Confess this sin and ask Him to cleanse you with His precious blood. The blood of Christ is all the evidence you need to present to the Judge of all to obtain a verdict of forgiveness. In so doing, you continue in right standing with the Judge of all in the courts of Heaven. Begin to see yourself as a *saint*, and not a *sinner.* A 'righteousness consciousness' is the gold standard you are to pursue.

"I am a saint who occasionally sins" needs to be your mindset.

Let's Internalize and Apply!

1. Who is for you in the courts of Heaven?

   ____

   ____

2. What speaks loudly on your behalf in the courts of Heaven?

   ____

   ____

3. True/False: Faith in God is your belief and acceptance of the finished work of Christ for your salvation that is recognized in the courts of Heaven.

4. What is meant by the two-fold work of Christ?

   ____

   ____

5. True/False: The ultimate goal of fully accepting and implementing the *faith in God* principle is for you to adopt a *sin-consciousness* view of yourself.

6. True/False: You can genuinely say, "I no longer see myself as a sinner, but as a saint. . . who occasionally sins.

Chapter 13

Developing A Righteousness Consciousness

The outcome of the *faith in God* principle is that you no longer live life from a sin-consciousness view of yourself, but from a *righteousness-consciousness* view. God does not have a *sin consciousness* view of you, because Jesus dealt with your sin once and for all. Rather, the Godhead has a *righteousness conscious*ness or view of you made in Their image and likeness. In fact, it was the Father's desire that you have *"no more consciousness of sin,"* because that is not your new identity (Heb. 10:2).

The Lord is working to remove a 'sin-consciousness' view from you and replace it with a 'righteousness consciousness' view. This is the only way your Father sees you and works with you. The Father, Jesus, and Holy Spirit only see one version of you, as a new man or creation in Christ. God only speaks to you in line with your identity in Christ. Let's learn how you can partner with Him in this transforming process.

The New Testament idea of *confess* simply means "to agree and say what God says." When you "confess," you are releasing testimony in the courts of Heaven that agrees with what the Father declares about you. One practical approach we recommend is for you to say what God says about you by declaring the *"You Saids."* Talk about yourself – the 'real' you -- the way God sees you and talks about you in His Word. For example, you can declare:

"Heavenly Father, ***You said***:

> I am the righteousness of God in Christ Jesus.
>
> I am completely forgiven of all my sins."
>
> I am complete, perfect, and holy as Jesus is.

The Father loves it when you speak His Word back to Him. Make it an on-going practice to believe, speak, and activate all that God believes and thinks about you.

Below you will find truth statements about you that reflect how your true identity is recognized in the courts of Heaven. Your identity in Christ consists of truth statements, each reflecting a unique facet of who you are as a *new man* in Christ. These truth statements fall into three clusters: I am Accepted, I am Secure, and I am Significant.

Declaring these truths releases testimony in the courts of Heaven on your behalf. It is a robust way to implement the *faith in God* principle.

I am Accepted

The identity statements below focus on your **acceptance** in Christ.

> "Father, I believe and confess these truths about me. *You said*:"

- I am *totally accepted* by God (Rom. 15:7; Eph. 1:5-6 NKJV); to the extent that the Father accepted the finished work of Jesus, He accepts me
- I am *reconciled* to God and *adopted* as His child (Rom. 5:11; Eph. 1:5)
- I am *chosen* by God, holy and dearly loved (Col. 3:12; I Pet. 2:9)
- I am *well pleasing* to God (Matt. 3:17; Mark 1:11); I am in Christ who was well-pleasing to His Father
- I am *approved by God* (I Thess. 2:4)
- I am a *friend* of God (John 15:15)
- I am *completely forgiven* of all of my sins – past, present, and future (I John 2:1-2; Col. 3:13; Heb. 9:12, 15; 10:10, 14)
- I am *free from condemnation* because Jesus has given me the gift of no-condemnation (Rom. 8:1, 34).
- I am the *righteousness of God* in Christ Jesus (Eph. 4:24; II Cor. 5:21).
- I am *holy* and without blame before God (Eph. 4:24; I Cor. 3:17; I Pet. 2:5, 9)
- I am *perfect, complete, and mature* as Jesus (Heb. 10:14; 12:23)
- I am a *new creation* in Christ and therefore a 3rd heaven creation. (II Cor. 5:17-18; Gal. 6:15)
- I am a *partaker of His divine nature* (2 Pet. 1:4)
- I am a *saint* (a "holy one") (Eph. 2:19; Rom. 1:7; Col. 1:2)
- I am a *masterpiece* (His "workmanship") (Eph. 2:10)
- I am *crowned* with *glory* and *honor* (Heb. 2:7)
- I am a *child* of the Most High God! (John 1:12; Rom. 8:16)

- I am *fully qualified* to share in the fullness of His inheritance (Col. 1:12).
- I am *redeemed* from the curse of the law, *purchased* by God (Gal. 3:13; I Pet. 1:18-19; I Cor. 6:19-20; Acts 20:28)
- I am *deeply and tenderly loved* by God (John 3:16; Jer. 31:3)
- I am *highly favored* (Eph. 1:6; Luke 1:28); in fact, I am *crowned with favor* (Prov. 4:9)
- I am *greatly blessed* and cannot be cursed (Eph. 1:3; Numb. 23:8, 20)
- I am a *joint heir* with Christ, sharing His inheritance with Him (Rom. 8:17)
- *I am sanctified* (positionally) as holy to God *(Heb. 2:11)*
- I am *fearfully* and *wonderfully made* (Psalm 139:14)
- I am a member of a *chosen race*, a *royal priesthood*, a *holy nation* (I Pet. 2:9-10)
- I am *justified* (declared not guilty) by the Blood of Christ (Rom. 5:9)
- I am a *victor*, not a victim. I have the *victory* through the Lord Jesus Christ (I Cor. 15:57)

I am Secure

The identity statements below focus on your **security** in Christ.

"Father, I believe and confess these truths about me". *"You said:"*

- I am *hidden with Christ* in God (Col. 3:3)
- I am *born again* and the evil one cannot touch me (I John 5:18).
- I am a *temple* in which God dwells (I Cor. 3:16)
- I am *united* to the Lord, one spirit with Him (I Cor. 6:17)
- I am *firmly rooted* and built up in Christ (Col. 2:7)
- I am a *living stone*, being built up in Christ as a spiritual house (I Pet. 2:5)
- I *cannot be separated* from the love of God (Rom. 8:35)
- I am securely *established* and *sealed* by God (2 Cor. 1:21, 22)
- I am *assured* that all things are working together for good (Rom. 8:28)
- I am a *citizen of heaven* (Phil. 3:20)

- I am *confident* that the *good work* God has begun in me *will be completed* (Phil. 1:6)
- I am the *head* and not the tail; I am *above only* and not beneath (Deut. 28:13)
- I am co-*crucified, co-buried, co-resurrected, co-ascended,* and *co-seated with Christ* in the heavenly realm and have 3rd heaven authority.
- I am *strong in the Lord* and in the strength of His might. (Eph. 6:10)

I have Significance

The identity statements below focus on your **significance** in Christ.

"Father, I believe and confess these truths about me". *"You said:"*

- I am *salt* and *light* in the world (Matt. 5:13-14)
- I am a *child of light* (Matt. 5:14: I Thess. 5:5)
- I am a *branch* of Christ's vine, a channel of His life (John 15:1, 5)
- I am a *member* of Christ's body (I Cor. 12:27)
- I am God's *coworker* (2 Cor. 6:1; I Cor. 3:9)
- I am *chosen* and *appointed* to *bear fruit* (John 15:16)
- I am a *minister* of reconciliation (2 Cor. 5:17 – 20)
- I am an *ambassador* of Christ (II Cor. 5:20)
- I am *more than a conqueror* (Rom. 8:37)
- I am *called* of God to fulfill my divine destiny (2 Tim. 1:9)
- I am a *king* and *priest* unto God (Rev. 1:6; 5:10)
- I am *transformed* from glory to glory into God's glory (2 Cor. 3:18)

Chapter 14

Putting Off, Putting On

(An Application Process)

We want to share with you a very simple way to apply the first two principles – *repentance from dead works* and *faith in God* – as one process. The process is called the Recircuiting Process.

Let's revisit Ephesians 4:22-25 which you learned about previously:

> *. . .lay aside the old self. . . and that you be renewed in the spirit of your mind, and put on the new self* [Greek anthropos = new man], *which in the likeness of God has been created in righteousness and holiness of the truth. Therefore, laying aside falsehood* [pseudo], *speak truth. . .*

Paul uses the language of putting off and putting on. It is the picture of *changing clothes.* As believers and followers of Jesus, we are to make sure we have the right clothing on before Him as we engage in the courts of Heaven. Just like in the natural, we do not put on one set of clothes over another, so we don't do this in the spirit. We must *undress to redress.* In other words, we must *put off* the old man and his deeds. The *old man* is the old nature whose desires are against God and His ways. When you were born-again, this *old man* died and was left buried in the grave. Consider yourself dead to sin and alive to God. The Father does.

Even though the old nature was crucified and left in the grave, we still have a mind that needs to be transformed by the Holy Spirit and the Word. Our mind and heart still retain a lot of wrong thinking about who God is, about our identity in Christ, and negative thoughts about ourselves -- all beliefs that carried over from our old nature. Our born-again spirit has been fully transformed but our soul has not. So our soul (mind, heart) must catch up to what has already transpired in our spirit. Putting off these wrong ways of thinking is like changing a set of clothes. In our mind, we must crucify the old and resurrect the new.

As a result of the *old man* dying, we must discard the ways of the old nature by actively renouncing and rejecting the old. The new nature in our spirit prompts us to love what God loves and to hate what God hates. We are now free to bring our behavior into agreement with God's nature and ways.

The Recircuiting process we are about to share is a *putting off* and a *putting on.* Here are important elements of the recircuiting process.

PUT OFF the imposter: Put off (that is, crucify) the falsehood (*pseudos* = lies, imposter, fake) notions of who you are. This means to *renounce* and *reject* them as not who you are. This is the repenting phase.

- *Actively* renounce and reject, and cut all ties with each false notion. Put them to death.

- *Root out* entrenched habits (i.e., critical words, quick to anger, tendency to be fearful).

If you have a deep-seated wound in your spirit from a prior experience that resulted in a vivid negative memory, you will need to *aggressively* root out that memory and replace it with the truth about your identity in Christ. This can be especially challenging if there is a strong emotional attachment associated with that memory.

Mistakes, labels from others, wrong attitudes, and negative self-talk do not belong to you. . . they belong to Jesus.

Put off wrong hearing – labels, lies.

Put off wrong believing, feelings and attitudes.

Put off wrong speaking – negative self-talk.

Put off wrong habits and practices.

In doing so, you are removing inaccurate perceptions, wrong beliefs, agreements, and attachments from your soul.

Your mistakes, labels from others, wrong attitudes, and negative self-talk do not belong to you. Jesus paid dearly for them, so they don't belong to you. They belong to Jesus, so put off these things and give them back to Him. He crucified and buried them for you, and He did not bring them through the resurrection. He only resurrected your new self which was raised in newness of life. Consider yourself dead to these negative things. In the future, be careful of the agreements that you consent to and speak.

Let's Discuss!

What are those things in your mind that you need to reject, renounce, and cut out?

What do you need to "put to death?"

The Father only sees one version of you – your new man. Your old self was crucified at the cross. Let's pray and reinforce this truth in the courts of Heaven:

> *Lord Jesus, as I stand before Your Courts, I thank You that the old man has died with You at the cross. When You died on the cross, the old man / old nature in me died with You. I now by faith discard this old man way of thinking like a set of unwanted clothes. The passions and desires associated with that old nature no longer have control over me. Thank You, Lord Jesus, that You now empower me to be clothed with the newness of Your nature and life. Amen!*

RENEW: To renew means to relearn. Actively renew your mind with the truth of who you are in your born-again spirit as found in the Word of God.[17] Renewing your mind in this manner implants the truth into your heart to replace the false.

PUT ON more of Your New Self: Speak out-loud what is true about you and the life within you. In faith, actively *announce*, *confess*, and *embrace* out-loud the truth about your identity in Christ. This is like *receiving* and being *fully clothed* with a new garment. As you do, the Father is UPGRADING you on the inside, taking you up higher into your identity.

Put on right hearing – based on your true identity in Christ.

Put on right believing and attitudes.

Put on right speaking – positive self-talk.

Put on right habits and a righteous lifestyle.

Now, you are believing right and making good agreements and attachments to your soul.

The Father is UPGRADING you on the inside, taking you up higher into your identity.

Clothed to Stand in His Courts

To operate as a priest before the Lord in His courts, you must wear the right clothes. Clothing is important in the spirit realm. We all are "wearing" something in the spirit realm. To function in the courts of Heaven requires the right attire.

---

[17] Ephesians 4:23 "*be renewed in the spirit of your mind. . .*"; Romans 12:2 "*be transformed by the renewing of your mind. .*"

Endeavor to be clothed with the "right garments" so you are recognized in the spirit world as one who can function there. We as kings and priests of our God are to have the right clothing for this function (Rev. 5:10). As we repent and stand before the Lord, His blood will cause us to have on the right garments, so that we may stand in His presence without fear and operate as His priests in His Courts.

You clothed yourself with the nature of Christ when you embraced a righteousness-consciousness view of yourself; you possess His divine nature (2 Pet. 1:3-4) to operate in the courts of Heaven. You must make sure that your thoughts and actions are in agreement with the new nature you have received.

Let's pray to put on the right clothes:

> *Lord, as I stand in Your Courts, I ask that I might be clothed with Your divine nature. I ask that I would be clothed with a robe of righteousness that would allow me to function as a king and priest before You in the spirit realm. Lord, take away any negativity and shame associated with me, and allow me to stand before You completely welcomed and recognized as Your son/daughter. I thank you that I stand before you accepted and pleasing to You as the result of the finished work of Christ. I am now clothed with the right garments provided for me through Your atoning blood. Amen!*

Let's Discuss!

What are some ways that you can form the new man in your mind and heart?

As a Christian, the spiritual realm recognizes who you are in Christ and what you carry. Heaven certainly does. The forces of darkness know who you are in Christ and the anointing you carry, which is why they fear you. Make it your aim to know who you are in Christ.

The Recircuiting Steps

Now let's implement the simple steps of *recircuiting* your mind. The first step is DIAGNOSIS. Ask the Lord two questions concerning the lies and truths regarding your identity. Take the time to listen to what the Lord says to you and write them down.

> What **lies** do I believe about my identity that I need to change?
>
> What's **true** about my identity?

Once you have answers and scriptures from the Lord, move on to the final step: the CURE.

For each lie about your true identity, you must repent, reject and renounce and then declare or announce what is really true from scripture. In so doing, you are making a new agreement.

Recircuiting Steps

DIAGNOSIS	CURE / REWIRING
Ask God 2 questions:	(*making new neuro-connections*)
What **LIES** do I believe about [my identity]? (failure, disappointed God, feel unworthy, etc.)	I **reject and renounce** the lie that ______.
What's **TRUE** about [my identity]? (success, God is proud of me, not disappointed in me)	I choose to believe and **declare and announce** that _____________.
	(*making new agreements*)

Now, you have intentionally made a new agreement in your mind and in faith you speak words of the new agreement into the spiritual realm and the physical realm. This sends a signal to your sub-conscious mind which begins to dissolve the negative neuropath (wrong belief) and begins to build the new neuropath. Choose to make only positive agreements with your words and mind.

This process physically recodes or rewires your brain. With the words of your new agreement, you are partnering with God to recode your thinking and feelings, which drives your actions, which then drives the new result (beliefs about yourself).

Let's Discuss!

Returning to the two question to ask God:

*What are the **lies**, wrong perceptions, and negativity that I have believed and agreed to that need to be renounced and rejected?*

*What is the **truth** about my identity that I need to embrace and declare that results in a new agreement and attachment?*

Examples

Let's look at examples of the recircuiting steps in action. Here is the first example.

From ***I Feel Rejected. . .*** to ***God Deeply Loves and Totally Accepts Me!***

Romans 15:7

Therefore, accept one another, just as Christ also accepted us to the glory of God.

Romans 5:5

The love of God has been poured out within our hearts through the Holy Spirit who was given to us.

I REPENT and RENOUNCE the lie that I am rejected, and ANNOUNCE the truth that God deeply loves me and He totally accepts me!

I declare that I am deeply loved by God!

I declare that I am totally accepted and fully pleasing to God!

From ***I Feel Depressed. . .*** to ***God Has Provided Me with Peace and Joy!***

Philippians 4:4

Rejoice in the Lord always; again I will say, rejoice!

Philippians 4:7

And the peace of God, which surpasses all comprehension, will guard your hearts and your minds in Christ Jesus.

Romans 15:13

Now may the God of hope fill you with all joy and peace in believing, so that you will abound in hope by the power of the Holy Spirit.

I REPENT and RENOUNCE all feelings of depression, and ANNOUNCE the truth that God has provided me with peace and joy!

I declare that I will rejoice in the Lord continually!

I declare that I choose to live a life filled with joy!

I declare that I have the peace of God which passes all understanding!

From ***My Future Seems Bleak. . .*** to ***God Has a Great Plan for My Life!***

Psalm 139:14, 16

I am fearfully and wonderfully made.

In Your book were all written the days that were ordained for me.

Jeremiah 29:11, 13

'For I know the plans that I have for you,' declares the Lord, 'plans for welfare and not for calamity to give you a future and a hope.' You will seek Me and find Me when you search for Me with all your heart.

Acts 13:36

For David. . . served the purpose of God in his own generation.

I REPENT and RENOUNCE the lie that God has a bleak future for me, and ANNOUNCE the truth that God is absolutely good and has a great plan and destiny for my life!

I declare that my destiny which You have written in Your destiny book about me in heaven will come to pass!

I choose to connect to my destiny!

I declare that Father God is absolutely good and has a good plan for my life!

I decree that I will fulfill my God-given destiny and assignment in this season!

I decree that I will serve and fulfill the purposes of God in my generation!

Let's Internalize and Apply!

1. In the Recircuiting steps, what are the two questions to ask the Lord in the Diagnosis step?

____

____

2. What are the two phases of the Cure (or Rewiring) step?

____

____

Section 5

The *Doctrine of Baptisms* Principle

"of *the doctrine of baptisms. . .*" Hebrews 6:2

In this section you will learn what is referred to as the doctrine of Baptisms. The doctrine of Baptisms should be regarded as one doctrine – as a whole with three necessary and related parts. What you experience in one baptism prepares you for the next one, and the three combined together equip you to live an overcoming life.

The word baptism in Greek is the word *baptisma* which means to dip, immerse, or submerge. Similarly, the verb form "to baptize" is the Greek word *baptizo* which is the action of submerging, baptizing, or dipping.

The doctrine of baptisms has three parts as noted in the chart below.

KIND OF BAPTISM	BAPTIZER	PERSON BAPTIZED	THE ELEMENT
Baptism Into Christ Spirit "In"	The Holy Spirit	Professing Believer	Into Body of Christ
Water Baptism	Christian Minister	Regenerated Believer	In water
Baptism in Holy Spirit Spirit "Upon"	Christ the Baptizer	Spirit-baptized Believer	In the One Holy Spirit

You have now entered into a covenant relationship with God as you co-identify with the death (repentance), burial (water baptism), and resurrection (life in the Spirit) of His Son, the Lord Jesus Christ. Through each baptism, the Holy Spirit produces distinct spiritual changes in you.

As you see, both the Holy Spirit and also the Lord Jesus Christ have a role in baptizing. The Holy Spirit and Christ are baptizers, but for different purposes. At one's conversion or salvation experience, the Holy Spirit is the baptizer, placing the believer into the Church, the Body of Christ. This will be explained further in the upcoming chapters.

There are biblical examples where all three of these types of baptism occurred in the same passage:

- On the day of Pentecost (Acts 2:37 – 38, 41)
- The Samaritan revival (Acts 8:5 – 17)
- The conversion, healing, and commissioning of the apostle Paul (Acts 9:3-18)
- The Gentiles saved and filled with Holy Spirit at Cornelius's home (Acts 10:44 – 48)
- The Ephesian disciples when apostle Paul arrived (Acts 19:1-6)

In Chapter 15 *Baptized into Christ*, you will learn about being baptized into Christ as a result of the new birth.

In Chapter 16 *Baptized in Water*, you will learn about water baptism as an important experience.

Finally, in Chapter 17 *Baptism in the Holy Spirit*, you will learn about the baptism in the Holy Spirit to receive an anointing for ministry.

Chapter 15

Baptized Into Christ

The first part of the doctrine of Baptisms is being baptized into the body of Christ.

When you receive Jesus Christ as your Savior (your conversion or salvation experience), the Holy Spirit baptizes or places you as a believer into the Body of Christ, the universal Church. I Corinthians 12:13 states this concisely: *For by one Spirit we were all baptized into one body.* The Holy Spirit is the one doing the baptizing, placing you into Christ.

The apostle Paul further explains it this way: *For all of you who were baptized into Christ have clothed yourselves with Christ* (Gal. 3:27). You are now taking on Christ's nature, becoming a member of His body, the Church. Paul also describes being baptized into Christ this way: *"Or do you not know that all of us who have been baptized into Christ Jesus have been baptized into His death?"* (Rom. 6:3).

Baptism into His death means your old sin nature was crucified and placed in the grave; but it was not resurrected when Christ was raised from the dead. The "dead" part of you was left in the grave, so you should consider the old nature of your spirit to be dead, and now alive to God because you received the new nature of Christ in your spirit. You are now *"clothed. . . with Christ."* Hence, there is only one version of you – the new man.

KIND OF BAPTISM	BAPTIZER	PERSON BAPTIZED	THE ELEMENT
Baptism Into Christ Spirit "In"	The Holy Spirit	Professing Believer	Into Body of Christ

As a result of the Holy Spirit baptizing you into Christ, you received Christ as your Savior who is living in you. But there are three other elements that you received as a part of the salvation "package": the fullness of the Godhead, the authority of the believer, and the fruit of the Spirit.

First, when you received Jesus Christ as Savior, you received what was in Him: the fullness of the Godhead. The Scriptures tell us that the Father was pleased that the fullness of Deity (the Godhead) dwelled in Christ.[18] This truth is a challenge to wrap our minds around, isn't it? Are you ready for this? As the Holy Spirit baptizes and places you into the Body of Christ, you too possess the three persons of the Godhead – Father, Son and Holy Spirit.[19] You have a layer or measure of all three members of the Godhead which were placed into your spirit when you received Christ!

For our purposes here, we will only focus on receiving Jesus and receiving Holy Spirit. At salvation, you have Jesus living in your spirit. The Holy Spirit also came **in** (*en* in Greek) you sealing the new birth in your spirit. You have both Jesus and Holy Spirit living *in* you as a result of the new birth The Holy Spirit in you witnesses with your spirit that you are a child of God and now develops the new nature of Christ in you.

> *You are. . .in the Spirit, if indeed the Spirit of God dwells* **in** [en] *you. But if anyone does not have the Spirit of Christ, he does not belong to Him. . . But if the Spirit of Him who raised Jesus from the dead dwells* **in** [en] *you, He who raised Christ from the dead will also give life to your mortal bodies through His Spirit who dwells* **in** [en] *you.* Rom. 8:9, 11 (bold and brackets added)

As a part of the new birth, you receive a *layer* or measure of the Holy Spirit along with receiving Jesus. (When you receive the baptism in the Holy Spirit, you receive the *fullness of the person* and the *power* of the Holy Spirit which you will learn about in an upcoming chapter.). At this stage, you receive a measure of the Spirit. Several terms are used to describe Holy Spirit baptizing you into Christ including being born again, salvation or saved, new creation in Christ, etc.

Let's Discuss!

How can you expand your understanding to accept that you have a layer or measure of each member of the Godhead living in you?

Second, you receive *authority* as part of the new birth, at conversion. *Authority* as a believer and the *power* of the Holy Spirit are received at different times and from

---

[18] See Colossians 1:19; 2:9

[19] Colossians 2:10 AMPC: "*And you are in Him, made full and having come to fullness of life [in Christ you too are filled with the Godhead – Father, Son, and Holy Spirit – and reach full spiritual stature].*

different experiences. You receive power when you are baptized in the Holy Spirit (or filled with the Holy Spirit).

> *But you will receive power* [dunamis in Greek] *when the Holy Spirit has come upon you. . .* Acts 1:8 (bracket added)

We will learn more about power in an upcoming chapter in this section.

John 1:12-13 records when your receive *authority*:

> *But as many as received Him, to them He gave the right [*exousia = right *or authority in Greek] to become children of God, to those who believe in His name, Who were born. . .of God.*

When you receive Christ as Savior, you receive authority as a believer. Notice that the basis of your authority in Christ is your close co-identity with the finished work of Christ in His crucifixion, burial, resurrection, ascension, and seating.

Jesus Christ	Me	
Crucified	*Co-crucified*	**Gal. 2:20** *I have been crucified with Christ* **Rom. 6:6** *our old self was crucified with Him*
Buried	*Co-buried*	**Rom. 6:4** *we were buried with Him through baptism into death*
Resurrected	*Co-resurrected*	**Rom. 6:4** *as Christ was raised from the dead through the glory of the Father, so we too might walk in newness of life* **Rom. 6:11** *consider yourselves. . . alive to God in Christ Jesus* **Eph. 2:4-5** *But God. . .made us alive together with Christ*
Ascended	*Co-ascended*	**Eph. 2:4, 6** *But God. . .raised us up with Him*
Seated	*Co-seated*	**Eph. 2:6** *and seated us with Him in heavenly places in Christ Jesus*

As Jesus was crucified, you are *co-crucified* with Him because of your close identity with Christ. As Jesus was buried, you are *co-buried* with Him. As Jesus was resurrected, you are *co-resurrected!* As Jesus ascended and was seated at the right hand of the Father in heavenly places, so too you are *co-ascended* and *co-seated* with Christ in heavenly places – far above all rule, and authority, and power, and dominion, and might! This is who you are!

It is not the case that Jesus was first crucified, buried, resurrected, ascended, and seated, and then, as an add-on, you and I were co-identified with Christ in these five ways. No, the Scripture is clear in the passages in the above chart that what happened to Jesus Christ happened *at the same time* positionally to you and me!

Your authority derives from the fact that you are co-seated at the right hand of the Father with Jesus! We cannot over-emphasize to you the importance of this truth. Picture yourself as co-seated with Jesus in heaven. The Father does.

Finally, the fruit of the Spirit was imparted into your spirit in *seed* form when you were *born* of the Spirit. The fruit were planted in your life as nine different *seeds* that are to be watered and cultivated until they grow to maturity.

> *But the fruit of the Spirit is love, joy, peace, patience, kindness, goodness, faithfulness, gentleness, self-control; against such things there is no law.* Galatians 5:22-23

Each fruit of the Spirit is activated as a by-product of your relationship with the Holy Spirit. The fruit of the Spirit are to infiltrate your nature and personality until they become your new nature and way of life.

In summary, then, the Holy Spirit places you into the Body of Christ, the universal Church, when you receive Jesus Christ as your Savior. At this same time, you also receive the fullness of the Godhead in your spirit, the authority of the believer, and the fruit of the Holy Spirit.

Let's Internalize and Apply!

1. When you are baptized into Christ, who does the baptizing? What are you baptized into?

   ____

   ____

2. In addition to receiving Christ into your spirit at salvation, what or who else did you receive?

____

____

3. At what point do you receive authority? What is a good Scripture reference?

____

____

4. What does it mean to be co-identified with Jesus Christ?

____

____

5. When did you receive the fruit of the Spirit deposited into your spirit? What did you receive?

____

____

Chapter 16

Baptism in Water

Baptism in water is the next step after you have received Jesus Christ as your Savior.

When you participate in water baptism, a Christian minister or leader is the baptizer, you are the person being baptized, and the element you are baptized into is water. You are now publicly identifying with the truth that you are dead to your sin nature and alive unto God.

KIND OF BAPTISM	BAPTIZER	PERSON BAPTIZED	THE ELEMENT
Water Baptism	Christian Minister	Regenerated Believer	In water

Baptism by immersion in water illustrates your identification with Christ's death, burial, and resurrection. Romans 6:4 – 7 describes this truth:

> *Therefore we have been buried with Him through baptism into death, so that as Christ was raised from the dead through the glory of Father, so we too might walk in newness of life.*
>
> *For if we have become united with Him in the likeness of His death, certainly we shall also be in the likeness of His resurrection, knowing this, that our old self was crucified with Him, in order that our body of sin might be done away with, so that we would no longer be slaves to sin; for he who has died is freed from sin.*

The action of being immersed in the water pictures your nature dying and being buried with Christ. When you are raised out of the water, you are symbolically resurrected—raised to new life in Christ to be with Him forever. The action of coming out of the water illustrates Christ's resurrection. Water baptism illustrates a spiritual cleansing for you, just as water cleanses your skin.

What is the proper mode of baptism?

The simplest answer to this question is found in the meaning of the word "baptize." It comes from a Greek word which means "to submerge in water." Therefore, baptism by sprinkling or by pouring is self-contradictory. Baptism, by its inherent definition, must be an act of immersion in water.

Baptism by immersion in water is an act of your obedience. It is a public proclamation of your faith in Christ and identification with His death, burial, and resurrection. You are now fully co-identified with Christ. Baptism by immersion is the only mode that fully illustrates this radical change.

In summary, water baptism by immersion is the biblical method of baptism because of its symbolic representation of the death, burial, and resurrection of Christ.

Why be baptized in water?

1. **Water baptism is commanded by Jesus.**

Baptism by immersion was commanded by Jesus when He said, *Go therefore and make disciples of all the nations, baptizing them in the name of the Father and the Son and the Holy Spirit"* (Matt. 28:19). These instructions specify that the church is responsible to teach what Jesus taught, make disciples, and baptize those disciples. These things are to be done everywhere ("all nations") until "*the end of the age*." So, if for no other reason, baptism has importance because Jesus commanded it.

You should be baptized out of obedience to and love for Jesus! In John 14:15, Jesus said, "*If you love Me, you will keep My commandments*." Water baptism is a command we are to obey.

Water baptism symbolizes your total trust in and reliance on the Lord Jesus Christ, as well as a commitment to live obediently to Him.

2. **Water baptism publicly expresses turning away from your old nature and embracing your new nature.**

Baptism is a picture of leaving our old life and becoming a new creation. The apostle Paul expressed this truth this way in 2 Corinthians 5:17: *Therefore if anyone is in Christ, he is a new creature; the old things passed away; behold, new things have come.* As you learned previously, the Father only sees one version of you – the new man! You are no longer your own but a temple of the Holy Spirit, which belongs to Christ (I Cor. 6:19).

3. Water baptism circumcises your heart.

The word *circumcise* means to cut away the enmity (hostility) that is in your heart. This frees you to more easily obey the Lord and welcome the presence of Holy Spirit into your life. Here is a description of the spiritual work of circumcision through water baptism:

> *In Him also you were circumcised with a circumcision not made with hands, but in a (spiritual) circumcision (performed by) Christ by stripping off the body of the flesh (the whole corrupt, carnal nature with its passions and lusts). (Thus you were circumcised when) you were buried with Him in (your) baptism, in which you were also raised with Him (to a new life) through (your) faith in the working of God (as displayed) when He raised Him up from the dead.* Colossians 2:11-12 AMPC

4. Water baptism expresses unity with all the saints.

Water baptism expresses unity with fellow saints in every nation on earth who are members of the Body of Christ. All Christians become one in Christ Jesus.

Water baptism is not a requirement for salvation.

Baptism by immersion, while the most Biblical mode of identifying with Christ, is *not* a prerequisite for salvation. This is best seen in the example of a saved man who was not baptized in water—the criminal on the cross. This self-confessed sinner acknowledged Jesus as his Lord while dying on a cross next to Him. The thief asked Jesus for salvation and was forgiven of his sins. Although he never experienced water baptism, at that moment he was placed into the Body of Christ; he then was raised to eternal life according to Christ's word (Luke 23:43).

Let's Internalize and Apply!

1. When you are baptized in water, into what are you identifying with?

   ____

   ____

2. What does immersion into water picture?

   ____

   ____

3. What does “coming up out of the water” picture?

4. What is the proper mode of water baptism?

5. Name two reasons to be water baptized?

Chapter 17

Baptism in the Holy Spirit

We have now come to the third and final component of the doctrine of Baptisms: the baptism in the Holy Spirit.

When you are baptized in the Holy Spirit, Jesus Christ is the baptizer, you as a believer are the person being baptized, and the element is the Holy Spirit. At this time, you receive the Holy Spirit "upon" to anoint you with power for witnessing and ministry.

KIND OF BAPTISM	BAPTIZER	PERSON BAPTIZED	THE ELEMENT
Baptism in Holy Spirit Spirit "Upon"	Christ the Baptizer	Spirit-baptized Believer	In the One Holy Spirit

As you are learning, being baptized in the Holy Spirit is a distinct experience from conversion (the new birth). R.A. Torrey, in his excellent book, *The Person and Work of the Holy Spirit*, captures this distinction well:

> It is evident that the baptism with the Holy Spirit is an operation of the Holy Spirit distinct from and additional to His regenerating work. . . A man may be regenerated by the Holy Spirit and still not be baptized with the Holy Spirit. In regeneration, there is the impartation of life by the Spirit's power, and the one who receives it is saved: in the baptism with the Holy Spirit, there is the impartation of power, and the one who receives it is fitted for service.[20]

To *have* the Spirit when you are born again is one thing, but to be *filled* with the Spirit is quite another thing. The first is *to regenerate*, the latter is *to empower*.

In Scripture, Jesus' first disciples were commanded to wait in Jerusalem to receive the baptism in the Holy Spirit (Luke 24:49). Jesus had been crucified but was very much alive. The disciples had witnessed all of this and had seen Jesus alive in His resurrected body. In addition, they had witnessed Him ascend into heaven! Wow! They really had a wonderful story to tell and they knew it! They were filled with joy and excitement, and

---

[20] R.A. Torrey, *The Person and Work of the Holy Spirit* (New York: Fleming H. Revell, 1910), 50

had a wonderful message to share with everyone. How could they keep this good news to themselves? They are about to explode! But they are commanded to say nothing. At least not say anything just yet.

These first disciples were not yet anointed and equipped to preach, to heal, or to cast out evil spirits. In Luke 24:49, Jesus said that the disciples needed to wait until they were endued or "clothed." The disciples needed to be clothed with both the *person* (the *Helper*) and the *power* of the Holy Spirit, which had not yet been given. They were not yet anointed, empowered, and equipped to be witnesses. The disciples needed to put on their *spiritual clothes* in order to minister the heart of God.

They had received the Holy Spirit's *indwelling* on resurrection evening,[21] but they still needed the *baptism in* the Holy Spirit. Fifty days after the disciples were born of the Spirit, they were baptized in the Holy Spirit on the Day of Pentecost (Acts 2:1-4).

As believers, we all receive a measure of Holy Spirit at conversion; it still remains that all of us must be filled with or baptized in the Holy Spirit. In receiving the baptism in the Holy Spirit, you receive the full Personhood and the Power of Holy Spirit. Holy Spirit is the *Person* with the *Power.*

Jesus the Baptizer

The Scripture clearly identifies Jesus Christ, the Anointed One, as the person of the Godhead who baptizes or immerses you and me into the Holy Spirit. To become the baptizer, Jesus had to first have Holy Spirit upon Him which occurred when *"the Holy Spirit descended upon Him in bodily form like a dove"* (Luke 3:22). John the Baptist declared of Jesus that *"He will baptize you with the Holy Spirit and fire"* (Luke 3:16). Jesus is the one who baptizes us into the Holy Spirit.

Jesus Himself declared in Acts 1:5 and 8 to the first disciples and to us today that you *"will be baptized with the Holy Spirit"* and *"will receive power when the Holy Spirit has come upon you; and you shall be My witnesses.*

So, the Holy Spirit proceeds to us from the Father through Jesus Christ the Son. Jesus said: *"When the Helper comes, whom I will send to you from the Father, that is the Spirit of truth who proceeds from the Father, He will testify about me"* (John 15:26). Jesus sent another helper or comforter just like Himself: the Holy Spirit. In effect, Jesus is saying, "If you love Me, then you will love the Holy Spirit also."

---

[21] See John 20:22

On the day of Pentecost, Peter, confirming that Jesus Christ is the Baptizer, stated *"Therefore having been exalted to the right hand of God, and having received from the Father the promise of the Holy Spirit, He has poured forth this which you both see and hear"* (Acts 2:33).

One Holy Spirit

It is important to understand that there is only *one* Holy Spirit, not one for the gift of eternal life and another for the gifts or the fruit of the Holy Spirit.

> *There is one body and one Spirit, just as also you were called in one hope of your calling.* Eph. 4:4

Both the gifts and fruit come from the one and same Holy Spirit. The fruit of the Spirit is just as divine and supernatural as the gifts of the Holy Spirit. There is one overall promise of the Holy Spirit that includes both His *indwelling* and His *infilling* or *empowering* of God's people.

There is only *one* Holy Spirit, not one for the gift of eternal life and another for the gifts or the fruit of the Holy Spirit.

Jesus identifies the Spirit's personhood as *"another Helper"* (John 14:16). The Greek *parakletos* is translated as Comforter, Helper, Counselor, or Advocate. Jesus himself was the first Paraclete. The apostle John says that *"we have an Advocate* [parakletos] *with the Father, Jesus Christ the righteous"* (I John 2:1). The Holy Spirit is our other *parakletos* or Helper.

An important clue is found in the Greek word for "another," *allos*, which means "another of the same kind." If you love Jesus, you will love the Holy Spirit also. Jesus was saying, "The Holy Spirit is another person like Me."

Speaking in Tongues

The initial sign or physical evidence of the baptism in the Holy Spirit is speaking in tongues.

Receiving the baptism in the Holy Spirit with speaking in tongues occurs when Holy Spirit comes **upon** *[epi* in Greek*]* you. You become a Spirit-baptized believer who is empowered with the *person* and *power* of the Holy Spirit for witnessing and ministry. This is a subsequent experience that is separate from, and after, you are born again (born of the Spirit).

> *Then there appeared to them divided tongues, as of fire, and one sat* ***upon*** [epi] *each of them. And they were all filled with the Holy Spirit and began to speak with other tongues, as the Spirit gave them the utterance.* Acts 2:3-4 NKJV (bold and bracket added)
>
> *But you will receive power when the Holy Spirit has come* ***upon*** [epi] *you; and you shall be my witnesses both in Jerusalem, and in all Judea and Samaria, and even to the remotest part of the earth.* Acts 1:8 (bold and bracket added)

Speaking in tongues is the initial physical evidence of the baptism in the Holy Spirit in the book of Acts. Let's look at the accounts in the book of Acts when believers were baptized in the Holy Spirit.

> *And there appeared to them tongues as of fire distributing themselves, and they rested on* [epi = upon] *each one of them. And they were all filled with the Holy Spirit and began to* <u>*speak with other tongues*</u>*, as the Spirit gave them utterance.* Acts 2:3-4 (bracket, underline added)
>
> *While Peter was still speaking these words, the Holy Spirit fell upon* [epi] *all those who were listening to the message.* **. . .** All the circumcised believers who came with *Peter were amazed, because the gift of the Holy Spirit had been poured out on the Gentiles also. For they were hearing them* <u>*speak with tongues*</u> *and exalting God.* Acts 10:44-46 (bracket, underline added)
>
> *And when Paul had laid his hands upon them, the Holy Spirit came on* [epi] *them, and they began* <u>*speaking with tongues*</u> *and prophesying.* Acts 19:6 (bracket, underline added)

In Acts 2 on the day of Pentecost, notice that the physical evidence of the baptism in the Holy Spirit was not the fire, or the wind, or the noise, but speaking in tongues. God gives a physical and audible proof of you having received the baptism in the Holy Spirit. Speaking in tongues is implied in Acts 8:15-17 (Samaritans received) and Acts 9:17 (Paul filled with the Holy Spirit).

Speaking in tongues has both public benefits and private benefits which are beyond the scope of this book. To learn more about the baptism in the Holy Spirit, please check out our book entitled, *The Present-Day Ministry of the Holy Spirit.* To learn more about the benefits of speaking in tongues, please see our book, *Downloading Heaven's Resources.*

Let's Discuss!

The baptism in the Holy Spirit is received by the laying on of hands by another Spirit-filled believer or directly asking Jesus to baptize you in the Holy Spirit. If you have not received the baptism in the Holy Spirit yet, why not get alone with Jesus right now and ask Him to baptize you in the Holy Spirit? Tell Him you want to speak in tongues. Then open your mouth and begin to speak in tongues out loud.

John the Baptist tells us in the gospels that Jesus "*will baptize you with the Holy Spirit and fire*" (Luke 3:16). You likely have heard the phrase, "tested by fire." One of the works of the baptism in the Holy Spirit is to purify you by burning away impurities which hinder your growth. God uses this baptism of fire, often called *sanctification*, to discipline us to strengthen the parts of our character which are weak. Jesus fans the flame of His Spirit within you in the form of trials, tribulations, trouble, persecution. This fire, in part, further develops the fruit of the Spirit (Gal. 5:22-23) and the eight kingdom traits (the "blessed" statements of Matthew 5:3-12) within you. This process accelerates becoming a mature son or daughter. The process is not enjoyable, but it is necessary.

> *For whom the Lord loves He disciplines, and He scourges every son whom He receives. (*Hebrews 12:6)
>
> *Every branch in Me that does not bear fruit, He takes away; and every branch that bears fruit, He prunes it so that it may bear more fruit.* (John 15:2)

The word "prunes" in John 15:2 means to *un-mix*; we have allowed some things of the flesh or the world to mix with the things that are holy in our lives. The flame of the Spirit is pressing you to un-mix or cut away those things that do not belong in your heart. This process of correction and discipline also adjusts your will and attitudes so that you become a partaker of God's holiness. This baptism of fire experience draws you closer to the Father's heart and is for your own good. God deals with you as a son, as one of His own, who belongs to Him and not as an illegitimate child (Heb. 12:8). He treats you as a disciple, as a learner. He disciplines us for our profit.

Let's Recap: Why Receive the Baptism in the Holy Spirit?

The fullness of the Spirit is essential to fulfilling the purpose and mission to which God has called you. The importance and need of your receiving the baptism in the Holy Spirit after conversion is shown by the following.

God has provided us with the gift of the Holy Spirit.

> The Father provided the prophetic promise (Luke 24:49; Acts 1:4; 2:33) of the prophetic gift of the Holy Spirit so that we would be His prophetic mouthpiece to lost people.

Jesus Himself received the baptism in the Holy Spirit.

> When Jesus Christ came out of the waters of baptism, He received the "Spirit upon" with power in the form of a dove and was now empowered for ministry in the power of the Holy Spirit (Luke 3:21-22). In Luke 4:18, He read from Isaiah 61 that "the Spirit of Lord is upon Me because He anointed me. . ." Christ means, "the *anointed one*."

Jesus commanded His disciples not to proceed without the "Spirit upon" them.

> The key is that it was His command (Luke 24:49; Acts 1:4). Of the 500 disciples who heard the command, 380 did not heed the command and did not receive. Only 120 heeded His command.

All of Jesus' disciples who obeyed His command (to not proceed without the Holy Spirit) did receive the Spirit.

> The disciples all received the baptism in the Holy Spirit and were filled, and spoke in tongues as the Spirit enabled them (Acts 2:1-4).

*The baptism in the Holy Spirit effected the conversion of 3,000 people on the day of Pentecost (*Acts 2:41).

The baptism in the Holy Spirit enabled the apostles to fill Jerusalem with their teaching (Acts 5:28)

The Spirit baptism enabled the apostles to perform supernatural signs and wonders.

The Spirit baptism enabled believers to carry the Gospel to every person of their generation (Col. 1:6, 23; Acts 17:6).

The Spirit-baptized disciples led their converts into the Spirit's baptism (Acts 8:14-15).

It was the norm for the churches to be Spirit-baptized congregations.

All believers are commanded to be filled with the Holy Spirit (Eph. 5:18; Matt. 28:19). *Being baptized in the Holy Spirit was a part of obeying fully.*

All believers are to be "filled with the Spirit." Jesus, who possesses all authority in heaven and earth, commanded believers to "teach others to observe all that He commanded you" which includes the command to receive the Spirit baptism. Acts 5:32 says, ". . .the Holy Spirit, who God has given to them that obey Him."

Let's Internalize and Apply!

1. Who baptizes you in the Holy Spirit?

____

____

2. What are you baptized into?

____

____

3. From whom does the Holy Spirit proceed?

____

____

4. True/False: There is one Holy Spirit for the gift of eternal life, another for the gifts of the Spirit, and yet another for the fruit of the Holy Spirit.

5. What is the initial, physical sign that you have received the baptism in the Holy Spirit?

____

____

6. True/False: When the Holy Spirit comes *upon* you, you are empowered with the *person* and *power* of the Holy Spirit for witnessing and ministry.

The *Laying On Of Hands* Principle

The principle of laying on of hands is very different from the other five principles. As you are learning, these six principles are really big ideas in the Christian faith. It is interesting that the laying on of hands is elevated to one of these principles that we need to master to go onto maturity.

The laying on of hands can be instrumental when imparting the Holy Spirit and His gifts upon believers, in ordination to ministry, in marriage, anointing with oil for healing the sick, in the dedicating and blessing of children, and in asking God's blessing and protection upon an individual.

In chapter 18, *The Laying on of Hands*, you will learn of the ways to minister the biblical practice of laying on of hands.

Chapter 18

Laying on of Hands

The principle or doctrine of laying on of hands is the belief and scriptural practice that spiritual power or qualities can be transferred from one believer to another by laying one's hands upon that individual. There are examples of the laying on of hands in both the Old Testament and in the New Testament. "Laying on of hands" is a biblical action and practice that God honors.

As a believer, you have something to give when you lay hands on another to bless them in some way. As we learned previously, you carry the fullness of the Godhead, and the Lord may prompt you to release a portion of what you carry to another person. You can impart the Holy Spirit and spiritual gifts, healing to the sick, install leaders, or bless and strengthen others as you lay your hands upon them and pray.

When you received Christ as Savior and became a new creation, you received a *deposit* of the anointing of the Spirit; that is, *"you have an anointing from the Holy One"* (I John 2:20). When you receive the baptism in the Holy Spirit, Christ, the Anointed One, gives you the *fullness* of the anointing that you can release to others (I Cor. 2:1:21-22 AMPC). Whether you have a deposit and/or the fullness of the anointing, you carry an endowment of the Spirit to bless others through the laying on of hands.

The words you speak or pray when you lay your hands on someone is very important. With your words, you can decree and release life, blessing, grace, destiny, and healing to the person to whom you are ministering.[22] The Lord may also give you a prophetic word to release over that person.

Impart the Baptism in the Holy Spirit

In the book of Acts, we see the baptism in the Holy Spirit with speaking in tongues imparted to recipients when hands are laid on them. For example, in Acts 8, after Philip proclaimed Christ to the city of Samaria, Peter and John came from Jerusalem to Samaria and *"began laying their hands on them, and they were receiving the Holy Spirit"* (v. 17).

In Acts 19 when the apostle Paul came to Ephesus to launch what would become the Ephesian revival, he met a small group of believers and asked them if they had received

---

[22] See Proverbs 15:4; James 3:10; Colossians 4:6; Psalm 139:16; Proverbs 12:18

the Holy Spirit. These believers had not yet received, so "*when Paul had laid his hands upon them, the Holy Spirit came on them, and they began speaking with tongues and prophesying*" (Acts 19:6).

There are other instances where the baptism in the Holy Spirit was received without the laying on of hands.

Imparting of Spiritual Gifts

All believers receive a measure of the Holy Spirit at salvation. However, when you receive the baptism in the Holy Spirit, He imparts other spiritual gifts that enable you to be an effective minister for Christ. Spiritual gifts include any of the nine gifts of the Spirit listed in 1 Corinthians 12: word of wisdom, word of knowledge, faith, gifts of healing, miracles, prophecy, distinguishing of spirits, tongues, and interpretation of tongues.

We see this in the example of Timothy receiving a certain spiritual gift to enable him to be an effective minister. The gift was imparted to Timothy through the laying on of hands by Paul and the other spiritual leaders. Paul wrote:

> "*Do not neglect the spiritual gift within you, which was bestowed on you through prophetic utterance with the laying on of hand by the presbytery*" (I Timothy 4:14).
>
> "*For this reason I remind you to kindle afresh the gift of God which is in you through the laying on of my hands*" (2 Timothy 1:6).

Paul was keenly interested in the life and ministry of Timothy, and he wanted to make sure that Timothy used the gift he had been given effectively, for the glory of God. Paul wanted Timothy to experience the fullness of God's gift.

The gifts you receive from the Lord through the infilling of the Holy Spirit are not given to you fully developed but need to be strengthened and matured through use. You will need to "*kindle afresh the gift*" or stir up your spiritual gifts as Timothy did. Timothy was told to not let his spiritual gift grow cold through disuse; he was to "stir it up" and keep the fire going.

You stir up the gift by *using* the gift you've been given. You stir up the gift by speaking in tongues on a regular basis. You stir up the gift by growing the fruit of God's nature in your life: love, joy, peace, patience, kindness, goodness, faithfulness, gentleness and self-control (Gal. 5:22-23). We keep the gift ablaze by not letting our spiritual vitality grow cold or, worse, lukewarm, as the church in Laodicea had done (Rev. 3:15-16). We fan the flames of faith by continuing to keep in step with the Spirit, following the Holy Spirit's direction and guidance in every part of our lives. We stir up the gift by not quenching or neglecting the Spirit of God, but allowing Him to thrive in us like a living, blazing fire.[23]

Signs and wonders can also manifest through the laying on of hands as was illustrated in Acts 5:12: *"At the hands of the apostles many signs and wonders were taking place among the people."*

Imparting Divine Healing

You can lay your hands on those who are sick or diseased and command healing to flow into their body. Jesus certainly laid His hands on many and imparted divine healing into their bodies. In fact, Jesus said that one of the key signs that you are a believer in Christ is you *"will lay hands on the sick, and they will recover"* (Mark 16:18).

There are numerous examples of Jesus healing such as:

- A synagogue leader asked Jesus to *"lay Your hands on her, so that she may get well and live"* (Mark 5:23, 41-42)
- The people of Decapolis asked Jesus to lay His hands on a man who was deaf to heal him (Mark 7:32-35)
- Jesus entered Capernaum *"laying His hands on each one of them"* with various diseases and healed them (Luke 4:40)

Likewise, here are a couple of examples where the first disciples released healing.

- Paul healing the father of Publius who was suffering from a fever and dysentery by praying and laying his hands on him to heal him (Acts 28:8).
- Peter healing the lame man at the gate Beautiful who had been lame from birth (Acts 3:6-8).

When we are seriously ill or sick, the apostle James exhorts us to call for the elders or leaders of our church to anoint us with oil and release healing to flow into our body (James 5:13-16). Laying on of hands typically occurs when anointing oil is applied for healing.

---

[23] See 1 Thessalonians 5:19; 1 Timothy 4:14

Impart Blessing and Strength to Others

One of the most powerful ways to bless another believer is to lay your hands upon them and speak words of blessing over them. We see laying on of hands to bless others modeled by Jesus when He took the children *"in His arms and began blessing them, laying His hands on them"* and He said, *"Permit the children to come to Me; do not hinder them; for the kingdom of God belongs to such as these"* (Mark 10:15-16). A common example of laying on of hands is when a baby or a child is dedicated to the Lord.

If you have children or grandchildren, please consider placing your hand on their head or shoulder periodically and decreeing words of life, blessing, and destiny over them. It can be as simple as "I speak God's blessing on you today" or "May peace and blessing be upon you" or "I bless you in the name of the Lord." Or "May you fulfill your divine destiny that God has for you." The Lord may also give you a prophetic word to speak over them. Consider speaking the blessing in Numbers 6:24 – 26 over them.

The laying on of hands can also have a strengthening effect on believers so that they can be more firmly established in their faith in Jesus Christ. We all go through tough times in our Christian journey and need our brothers and sisters to encourage and strengthen *"the hands which hang down and the feeble knees"* (Heb. 12:12 NKJV). Laying on of hands with prayer is a powerful way to impart strength and encouragement whether you are ministering to others or others are ministering to you.

We see this way of encouragement modeled by the apostles in the first century church when many believers were under strong persecution. The apostle Paul with Barnabas, in their missionary travels, would circle back to the church plants to strengthen and encourage the faith of these new believers. We read about this when Paul and Barnabas returned to Lystra, Iconium, and Antioch *"strengthening the souls of the disciples, encouraging them to continue in the faith, and saying, 'Through many tribulations we must enter the kingdom of God'" (Acts 14:22).* Sometime later in Antioch, prophets Judas and Silas, *"encouraged and strengthened the brethren with a lengthy message"* (Acts 15:32). This seems to infer that prayer and laying on of hands strengthened and encouraged these believers.

Conferring an Office or Assignment of Ministry

The last application we will learn about is when church leaders are installed into a position of leadership.

The term ordination comes to mind when we think of setting a person in a place of leadership in a church. The definition of *ordination* is a setting in place or an appointment, often granting a level of responsibility and authority. Ordination has two facets: (1) a recognition of calling by church leadership and the people and (2) the laying on of hands to install or commission into a ministry.

Acts 13 provides a good example of a ministerial appointment: *"While they were ministering to the Lord and fasting, the Holy Spirit said, 'Set apart for Me Barnabas and Saul for the work to which I have called them.' Then, when they had fasted and prayed and laid hands on them, they sent them away* (vv. 2-4). In this passage, we note the following facts:

1. It is God Himself who calls a person to the ministry and qualifies them with gifts (Acts 20:28; Eph. 4:11)

2. The members of the church recognize God's clear leading and embrace it

3. With prayer and fasting, the church lays hands on Paul and Barnabas to demonstrate their commissioning

4. God works through the church, as both the church and the Spirit are said to "send" ones to minister.

When God calls and qualifies a person for the ministry, it will be apparent both to that man or woman and to the rest of the church. It is the duty of the church elders, together with the congregation, to recognize and accept the calling. After that, a formal commissioning ceremony—an ordination service—is appropriate (although by no means mandatory). Typically the ceremony involves the laying on of hands. The ordination ceremony itself gives public recognition to God's choice of leadership.

It's important to note that the laying on of hands by church leadership can impart an anointing of the Spirit from one leader to another. We see examples of this in scripture. In the passage in Acts 13 above, we see an impartation into Paul and Barnabas to function as apostles.

In Numbers 11, Moses lays his hands on the 70 elders imparting into them the anointing to help him govern the children of Israel:

Then the Lord came down in the cloud and spoke to him: and He took of the Spirit who was upon him [Moses] *and placed Him upon the seventy elders. And when the Spirit rested upon them, they prophesied. But they did not do it again (v. 25).*

As a concluding example, we read of Moses in Numbers 27 conferring a portion of his anointing, spirit, and wisdom upon Joshua to be his successor:

> *"So the Lord said to Moses, 'Take Joshua the son of Nun, a man in whom is the Spirit, and lay your hand on him.*
> *You shall put some of your authority on him, in order that all the congregation of the sons of Israel may obey him.*
> *Then he laid his hands on him and commissioned him, just as the LORD had spoken through Moses. (vv.18, 20, 23).*

A Word of Caution

First Timothy 5:22 advises us, "*Do not lay hands upon anyone too hastily and thereby share responsibility for the sins of others: keep yourself free from sin."* The thought here is not so much in cautioning the physical action of laying on of hands but to urge care in bestowing the responsibility of spiritual leadership (however it is done). It is not to be done "suddenly" or without due consideration.

Internalizing and Applying!

1. What is the principle of laying on of hands?

   ____

   ____

2. When you lay hands on another person, what are some examples of what you can impart?

   ____

   ____

3. True/False: You can lay your hands on those who are sick or diseased and command healing to flow into their body.

4. True/False: One of the most powerful ways to bless another believer is to lay your hands upon them and speak words of blessing over them.

5. The laying on of hands can also have a _______________ effect on believers so that they can be more firmly established in their faith in Jesus Christ.

6. True/False: The laying on of hands by church leadership can impart an anointing of the Spirit from one leader to another.

Section 7

The *Resurrection of the Dead* Principle

The Bible is clear that this present life is not all that there is and that there is a resurrection awaiting all of us. Daniel 12:2 summarizes the two very different fates facing mankind:

> *"Many of those who sleep in the dust of the ground will awake, these to everlasting life, but others to disgrace and everlasting contempt."*

Everyone will be raised from the dead, but not everyone will share the same destiny.

In Chapter 19 *Resurrection of the Righteous*, you will learn about the wonderful experience that awaits all believers in Christ. This is the hope of the ages for those who belong to God.

In Chapter 20 *Eternal State of the Believer*, you will learn about what heaven will be like for the believer. It is glorious!

In Chapter 21 *Resurrection of the Unjust*, you will learn about the terrible fate of those who have chosen to not put their faith in the finished work of Christ. It is a fate of eternal separation from the presence and love of the Father.

Chapter 19

Resurrection of the Righteous

The Bible is clear that there is a resurrection awaiting all of us. While death is the end of physical life, it is not the end of human existence. God made you and me eternal beings. We are a three-part being consisting of a spirit, soul, and body. God has put eternity in the soul of each person. Paul wrote to the Corinthians that *"if there is a natural body, there is also a spiritual body"*. We are *"sown a natural body but raised a spiritual body."*[24]

Jesus stated that there is a resurrection for the righteous and a resurrection for the unrighteous:

> *"an hour is coming, in which all who are in the tombs will hear His voice, and will come forth; those who did the good deeds to a resurrection of life, those who committed the evil deeds to a resurrection of judgment"* (John 5:28-29).

All of us – whether a believer in Christ or not – have a fate after we die and will give an account of how we lived our life here.

The First Resurrection

All Christians will participate in the *"first resurrection"*(Rev. 20:5-6). The first resurrection is the raising of the physical bodies of all believers. Jesus called this the *"resurrection of the righteous"* (Luke 14:14).

The resurrection of our body is the hope that we have of the *"redemption of our body"* (Rom. 8:23). Previously, we learned about the Salvation Triangle where the finished work of Christ purchased our *redemption* with His own blood (I Pet. 1:18-19). Christ's redemptive work includes our spirit, soul, and physical body. When we receive Jesus as our Savior, we are born of the Spirit and our *spirit* is redeemed (John 3:6). This is when salvation comes to our spirit. Our *soul* is redeemed, in a sense, as we are transformed by the renewing our minds with the Word of God. But our focus here is on the redemption of our bodies.

When you received Jesus as Savior, you also received a measure of the Holy Spirit. As such, you received the *"first fruits of the Spirit,'* a down payment that your body will be

---

[24] See I Thessalonians. 5:23; Ecclesiastes 3:11; I Corinthians 15:44

resurrected. The first fruits of the Spirit is a pledge that your body will be made like the glorified body of Christ. The Holy Spirit is your seal or guarantee of a coming day when your body will also be redeemed.[25]

The Bible teaches that there will be not one resurrection but a series of resurrections. The "*first resurrection*" takes place in several *stages*.

Stage 1 – The First-Fruits Resurrection of Jesus

The first stage of the first resurrection was the resurrection of Jesus Christ. It is documented in each of the four Gospels[26], cited several times in Acts[27], and mentioned repeatedly in the letters to the churches[28]. Much is made of the importance of Christ's resurrection in I Corinthians 15:20 and 23:

> *But now Christ has been raised from the dead, the first fruits of those who are asleep. . . But each in his own order: Christ the first fruits, after that those who are Christ's at His coming.*

Christ's resurrection is the "*first fruits*" or guarantee to every Christian that he or she will also be resurrected. Christ's resurrection is also the basis of the Christian's certainty that all people who have died will one day be raised to face a fair and even-handed judgment by Jesus Christ:

> *God. . .has fixed a day in which He will judge the world in righteousness through a Man whom He has appointed, having furnished proof to all men by raising Him from the dead"* (Acts 17:30-31)

Christ Jesus is not only the first fruits from the dead, but He will also be the judge of believers at the Judgment Seat of Christ.

> *For just as the Father raises the dead and gives them life, even so the Son also gives life to whom He wishes. For not even the Father judges anyone, but He has given all judgment to the Son.* (John 5:21-22).

---

[25] See Romans 8:23; Philippians 3:20-21; Ephesians 1:13-14; 4:30
[26] See Matthew 28; Mark 16; Luke 24; and John 20
[27] See Acts 1:22; 2:31; 4:2, 33; 26:23
[28] See Romans 1:4; Philippians 3:10; 1 Peter 1:3

Stage 2 – The Resurrection of the Church

The second stage will be the resurrection of "*the dead in Christ*" at the Lord's return for His Church:

> *For the Lord Himself will descend from heaven with a shout, with the voice of the archangel and with the trumpet of God, and the dead in Christ will rise first. Then we who are alive and remain will be caught up together with them in the clouds to meet the Lord in the air, and so we shall always be with the Lord.* (I Thessalonians 4:16-17).

Jesus will return and meet believers in the air. The dead will rise first, those who are alive will follow, and we will all be with Him for eternity. This event is what we now call the Rapture, Jesus coming *for* his saints. The word *rapture* is not found in our English Bibles but comes from the Latin word for "caught up" in verse 17. At this *catching up,* we receive new bodies. When the Corinthian church asked what kind of bodies we would receive, Paul explained that it is a mystery:

> *Behold, I tell you a mystery; we will not all sleep, but we will be changed, in a moment, in the twinkling of an eye, at the last trumpet; for the trumpet will sound, and the dead will be raised imperishable, and this mortal must put on immortality.* . . (I Corinthians 15:51 – 53)

In Romans 8:11, Paul describes the role of the Holy Spirit in this mysterious transformational process: *But if the Spirit of Him who raised Jesus from the dead dwells in you, He who raised Christ Jesus from the dead will also give life to your mortal bodies through His Spirit who dwells in you.* Paul explains that believers will be raised from the dead with "spiritual bodies" in contrast to the "natural bodies" that die. This does not mean we will have immaterial bodies; rather, our bodies will be glorified and imperishable, unlike our present bodies. This is a mystery to us now but will be revealed on that day.

The resurrection from the dead for one who is a new creation in Christ is a *bodily resurrection* – where your physical body rejoins the spirit and soul. Earlier in I Corinthians, Paul wrote regarding the change to our bodies:

> *It is sown a perishable body, it is raised an imperishable body; it is sown in dishonor, it is raised in glory; it is sown in weakness, it is raised in power; it is sown*

a natural body, it is raised a spiritual body. If there is a natural body, there is also a spiritual body (I Corinthians 15:42 – 44).

Our resurrected bodies will not be entirely different from what they are today. The nature of Jesus' resurrected body suggests what our bodies will be like. The identity will be maintained. Recall that the disciples recognized Jesus after His resurrection. These things we do know about our resurrected body:

1. our new spiritual body will have a continuing identification with the old physical body
2. we will still be individuals in our new bodies, and
3. our new bodies will be perfect.

All those who have placed their trust in Jesus Christ during the church age and have died before Jesus' return will be resurrected at this *"catching up."* The church age began on the day of Pentecost and will end when Christ returns to take believers back to heaven with Him. The apostle Paul explained that not all Christians will die, but all will be changed, i.e., given resurrection-type bodies, some without having to die. Christians who are alive and those who have already died will be caught up to meet the Lord in the air and be with Him always.

Stage 3 – The Resurrection of the Martyrs at the End of the Tribulation

Another great resurrection will occur when Christ returns to earth (His second coming) at the end of the tribulation period: the resurrection of the martyrs.

During the tribulation period, millions of people left behind on earth will come to their senses during this time and will trust in Jesus as their Savior. Tragically, most of them will pay for their faith in Jesus by losing their lives[29]. These believers in Jesus who die during the tribulation will be resurrected at Christ's return to reign with Him for a thousand years:

> *. . .And I saw the souls of those who had been beheaded because of their testimony of Jesus and because of the word of God. . . and they came to life and reigned with Christ for a thousand years.* (Revelation 20:4 – 5)

---

[29] Revelation 6:9–11; 7:9–17; 13:7, 15–17; 17:6; 19:1–2

In summary, all believers in God (in the Old Testament era) and all believers in Jesus (in the New Testament era) participate in the first resurrection, a resurrection to life. There is a wonderful blessing pronounced on those who participate in this resurrection: *"Blessed and holy is the one who has a part in the first resurrection. . .* (Rev. 20:6a).

Stage 4 – A Resurrection at the End of the Millennium?

There may be another resurrection of the righteous at the end of the millennium; it is implied in Scripture. It is possible that some believers will die a physical death during the millennium. Through the prophet Isaiah, God said,

> *No longer will there be in it an infant who lives but a few days,*
> *Or an old man who does not live out his days;*
> *For the youth will die at the age of one hundred*
> *And the one who does not reach the age of one hundred*
> *Will be thought accursed.* (Isaiah 65:20)

On the other hand, it is also possible that death in the millennium will only come to the disobedient. In either case, some kind of transformation will be required to fit believers' bodies during the millennium to live in a glorified body on the new heaven and new earth.

What will happen to those believers who were born during the millennium, trusted in Jesus, and continued to live in their natural bodies? Paul taught that flesh and blood, which is mortal and subject to decay, cannot inherit the kingdom of God. That eternal kingdom is inhabitable only by those with resurrected, glorified bodies that are immune to decay (1 Cor. 15:35–49). Presumably, these believers will be given resurrection bodies without having to die. Precisely when this happens is not explained, but, logically, it must happen somewhere in the transition from the old earth to the new earth.

An Intermediate State

Prior to the resurrection of our body, we are in an intermediate state as a believer. While it is a state without our resurrected body, it is a time of conscious joy in the presence of the Lord. The apostle Paul was looking forward to being *"absent from the body and to be at home with the Lord"* (2 Cor. 5:8). Today, the righteous who have died no longer wait in Abraham's bosom as did the Old Testament saints, because Jesus at His ascension "*led captive a host of captives*" and took the righteous to heaven to enjoy the presence of the

Lord.[30] (When you die, you will go directly to the presence of the Lord.) Here, the righteous are completely enamored with Jesus as He welcomes them to heaven!

Scripture reveals that our soul is conscious when the body dies and recognizes other people who have died (Luke 16:22-25). Though our spirit/soul is separated from our physical body (which is still in the grave), we have not entered our complete and final condition.

When our body is resurrected at the Rapture ("catching up"), our body and spirit/soul are reunited once again in order that our entire person may take on an imperishable state. Our natural environment has always been the presence of the Lord. The intermediate state for the believer is described as a condition of bliss and of rest.

Let's Internalize and Apply!

1. True/False: The first resurrection is the raising of the spiritual bodies of all believers.

2. What was the first stage of the first resurrection?

 ____

 ____

3. True/False: Christ's resurrection is the *"first fruits"* or guarantee to every Christian that he or she will also be resurrected.

4. Who will be the judge of believers at the Judgment Seat of Christ?

 ____

 ____

5. True/False: The second stage will be the resurrection of *"the dead in Christ"* at the Lord's return for His Church.

---

[30] See Luke 16:22; Ephesians 4:8

6. True/False: The resurrection from the dead for believers is a *bodily resurrection* – where your physical body rejoins the spirit and soul.

7. What three things do we know from scripture that will be true about our resurrected bodies?

   ____

   ____

8. What is the third stage of the first resurrection that will take place at the end of the tribulation period?

   ____

   ____

9. True/False: Prior to the resurrection of our body, believers are in an intermediate state as a believer that is a state of joy, bliss, and rest in the presence of the Lord.

True/False: The resurrection from the dead for believers [illegible]

[illegible]

What [illegible]

Chapter 20

Eternal State of the Believer

Our Bodies in Heaven

While the Bible doesn't describe in detail the glorified bodies we will receive in heaven, we do know that our bodies will be like that of Jesus' resurrected body. Remember, Jesus is the *"first fruits"* of the resurrection of our body. Our immortal glorified bodies will be imperishable, honorable, and powerful. They will be pure and undefiled, with no taint of sin. We will no longer be subject to the natural laws of gravity and the limitations of time and space. Our glorified bodies will be empowered by the Spirit and weakness will be no more.

While our earthly bodies are fit for this world, our resurrected body will be fit for eternity in heaven. We will possess glorified bodies especially suited for the new heaven and new earth.

Our existence in heaven will not be marred by bad memories of the old earth. No more sin, sickness, disease, curse, or death. Joy will swallow up all distress: *"All former things will not be remembered or come to mind"* (Is. 65:17).

Gender in Heaven

The question about gender in heaven is an interesting one. Some people say that since Jesus said we would be *"like the angels"* and not marry in heaven that people will be all one gender. However, the preponderance of Scripture indicates that we will retain our gender in heaven and that the resurrection of the body will not change one's gender. Males will be males in heaven, and females will be females.

> Males will be males in heaven, and females will be females.

In fact, there is nothing in the Bible that indicates people will lose or change their gender in heaven. The Bible implies that we will remain who we are in heaven, and gender is part of who we are. Gender is part of our very nature and affects the way we relate to each other and to God. Elijah and Moses appeared in glory as themselves (Matt. 17:3) and the post-resurrected Jesus was still a "he" (Luke 24:27). No one lost his gender in heaven. God created humanity "male and female" before the fall and gender was part of the "*very good*" creation (Gen. 1:27, 31). There is no reason to think that gender will be lost in heaven.

Family and Friends

Many people say that the first thing they want to do when they arrive in heaven is see all their friends and loved ones who have passed on before them. That will indeed be a blessed time as believers reunite for fellowship, worship God, and enjoy the glorious wonders of heaven. One of the blessings is that we will know our friends and family members in heaven, and we will be known.

Our ability to recognize people in the afterlife is suggested in several passages of Scripture. At the transfiguration of Christ, Moses and Elijah made an appearance, and they were recognizable (Matt. 17:3-4). Though they had departed this world centuries prior, both Moses and Elijah remained distinct persons who had not lost their identity. In Luke 16:19-31, Abraham, Lazarus, and the rich man are all recognizable after death.

The Bible declares that, when we arrive in heaven, we will "*be like Him* [Jesus]; *because we will see Him just as He is*" (I John 3:2). Just as our earthly bodies were of the first man, Adam, so will our resurrection bodies be like Christ's glorious body.[31] " Jesus was recognizable after His resurrection,[32] so it stands to reason that we also will be recognizable in our glorified bodies.

> Our resurrected bodies will be like Christ's glorious body.

Being able to see our loved ones is a glorious aspect of heaven. What a pleasure it will be to reunite with our loved ones and worship God with them in His presence for all eternity!

Clothing in Heaven

Angelic beings are described in the Bible as wearing some kind of garments. In Daniel's vision, the messenger (an angelic being) was "*dressed in linen, whose waist was girded with a belt of pure gold*" (Dan. 10:5). Similarly, the angel guarding Jesus' tomb was wearing garments: "*And his appearance was like lightning, and his clothing as white as snow*" (Matt. 28:3).

---

[31] I Corinthians 15:47; Philippians 3:21

[32] John 20:16, 20; 21:12; I Corinthians 15:4-7

The redeemed in heaven are also described as clothed. In Revelation 4:4, the twenty-four elders around the throne of God wear white clothing and have golden crowns. Revelation 3:5 says that those who belong to Christ will be "*clothed in while garments*" in heaven. We are clothed with the righteousness of Christ.[33] The Bible never hints that anyone in heaven is unclothed.

In our opinion, we will not be naked in heaven. When we get to heaven, we are pictured as being covered with "*white garments so that you may cloth yourself, and that. . .your nakedness will not be revealed*" (Rev. 3:18).

Let's Internalize and Apply!

1. True/False: Our resurrected body will be glorified bodies especially suited for the new heaven and new earth.

2. True/False: Scripture indicates that we will retain our gender in heaven and that the resurrection of the body will not change our gender.

3. In heaven, will we know our friends and family members, and be known by them?

   ____

   ____

4. True/False: Those who belong to Christ will be "clothed in while garments" in heaven.

---

[33] Galatians 3:27; 2 Corinthians 5:21

Chapter 21

Resurrection of the Unjust

What great rejoicing there will be for those included in the first resurrection. However, there will be great anguish for those who are summoned to the second resurrection. The Bible indicates that non-believers will also have resurrected bodies on the last day (Daniel 12:2).

The event which divides the first and second resurrections seems to be the millennial kingdom. The last of the righteous are raised to reign *"with Christ a thousand years"* (Rev. 20:4). But the *"rest of the dead* [that is, the wicked] *did not come to life* [for the second resurrection] *until the thousand years were completed"* (Rev. 20:5).

The Second Resurrection

The second resurrection is for those whose names are not found in the "book of life" and, as a result, are sentenced to the lake of fire. Those summoned to the second resurrection are the wicked who will be judged by Jesus Christ at the great white throne judgment prior to being cast into the lake of fire (explained further in chapter 23, *Judgment of the Unjust*). The second resurrection, then, is the raising of all unbelievers; and it is referred to as the "second death."[34] The second resurrection corresponds with Jesus' teaching of the *"resurrection of judgment"* (John 5:29).

So the resurrection of the unjust will occur at the end of Christ's millennial reign. The second resurrection will include all the unjust from all ages, together with those who die during the tribulation period and the millennium. God will judge all unredeemed humanity, in addition to Satan and the fallen angels (Rev. 20:10). The result is that those whose names are not found written in the book of life will be cast into the lake of fire.

Those going to hell will be eternally separated from God. This is why is it called the "second death" -- being cast into the lake of fire to be tormented for eternity, separated from God. This is the worst place to ever be in: permanent separation from the presence and love of the Father. (The presence of the Father was meant to be our natural

---

[34] Revelation 2:11; 20:6, 14; 21:8

environment for all time.) This is a place of outer darkness, a furnace of fire, weeping, torment, and gnashing of teeth.[35] The final destination of the unrighteous is *Gehenna* (in Greek), the everlasting lake of fire mentioned in Revelation 19 and 20.

The Unrighteous Dead Today

Today, the unrighteous dead remain in *Sheol* (*Hades* in Greek) until the time of the second resurrection at the end of the millennium. This interim place of waiting, *Sheol*, is also referred to as Abraham's bosom in Luke 16:22. Here they are suffering and tormented, experiencing unquenchable thirst and agony, even before their final destiny is pronounced at the great white throne judgment. Instead of being in a place of rejoicing, the unrighteous dead are in a place of anguish and darkness.

Let's Internalize and Apply!

1. Who is the second resurrection for?

   ____

   ____

2. What two events await those summoned at the second resurrection?

   ____

   ____

3. True/False: The second resurrection is also known as the second death.

4. True/False: The resurrection of the unjust will occur at the end of the tribulation period.

5. Today, where do the unrighteous dead remain until the time of the second resurrection?

   ____

   ____

---

[35] See Matthew 8:12; 13:42, 50; 22:13; 24:51; 25:30; see Luke 13:28.

Section 8

The *Eternal Judgment* Principle

We have now come to the last of the six principles: the *eternal judgment* principle. We all must give an account of our lives to the Lord.

Jesus has been given the authority to judge by the Father. In John 5:22-23, Jesus says, "*Not even the Father judges anyone, but He has given all judgment to the Son, so that all will honor the Son even as they honor the Father.*" Jesus will act as judge over believers and unbelievers.

Yes, Jesus came into the world to save those who put their trust in Him, but His coming also brought judgment (Jn. 9:39). Through His death and resurrection, Jesus brought judgment to Satan (John 12:31). He is also the righteous judge and will repay each person according to his deeds (Matt. 16:27; Rom. 2:6).

In Chapter 22, you will learn about the judgement of the righteous.

In Chapter 23, you will learn about the judgment of the unjust or unrighteous.

Chapter 22

Judgment of the Righteous

Those who have put their trust in Christ will participate in the first resurrection. We hope you are a Christian and will be included in this resurrection. This resurrection will begin with the "catching up" or the rapture of the Church[36] and end with the resurrection of the Tribulation martyrs: "*and they came to life and reigned with Christ for a thousand years. Blessed and holy is the one who has a part in this first resurrection; over these the second death has no power* (Rev. 20:4 – 6).

Those who take part in the first resurrection will go to the judgment seat of Christ.

Judgment Seat of Christ

The judgment seat of Christ is for believers only and will take place in heaven prior to the Millennial reign of Christ. Paul wrote to the Romans, "*For we shall all stand before the judgment seat of Christ* (Rom. 14:10 NKJV). He confirmed this to the Corinthians when he wrote, "*For we must all appear before the judgment seat of Christ, so that each one may be recompensed for his deeds in the body, according to what he has done, whether good or bad*" (2 Cor. 5:10).

"*So then each one of us will give an account of himself to God*" (Rom. 14:12). This judgment does not determine our salvation, which is by faith alone (Eph. 2:8-9); rather, it determines the rewards believers will receive.

First Corinthians 3:11 pictures Christ as our *foundation*: "*For no man can lay a foundation other than the one which is laid, which is Jesus Christ.*" The surrounding verses tell us that the Christian life is about building on that foundation.

> *Now if any man builds on the foundation with gold, silver, precious stones, wood, hay, straw, each man's work will become evident; for the day will show it because*

---

[36] See I Corinthians 15:22-23: I Thessalonians 4:16

> *it is to be revealed with fire, and the fire itself will test the quality of each man's work.*
>
> *If any man's work which he has built on it remains, he will receive a reward.*
>
> *If any man's work is burned up, he will suffer loss; but he himself will be saved, yet so as through fire.* (1 Corinthians 3:12-15)

You can build, on the foundation of Christ, with "*gold, silver, precious stones,*" or you can build with "*wood, hay or straw*" (verse 12). What you construct will be tested, as it were, by fire. Your worthless, shallow activity will not survive God's refining fire; only what is done for God's glory will last. Only what you build on the foundation of Christ will last and be rewarded. The things done in this life are only permanent (that is, carried with us into heaven) if they are built on the foundation, which is Christ. The judgment seat of Christ will reveal whether your building is permanent or temporary.

You will be rewarded based on your good works in Christ's service and your faithfulness to the Lord. You will give an account of your actions, inactions, words, thoughts, and motives. Were they truly a reflection of your position in Christ? So then, each of us will give an account of ourselves to God.

In the Greek, a single word is used for "judgment seat"; the word is *bema*.[37] A *bema* was a raised platform on which judges sat to view athletic games. Their job was to make sure contestants followed the rules and to present awards to the victors (I Cor. 9:24-27). The *bema* was never a place to reprimand the athletes or to punish them in any way. It was a place of testing and reward. In the same way, the *bema* of Christ will not be a place of condemnation or censure.

Christ will judge your work based on your words, actions, motives, and character. Your motives and faithfulness appear to be the most important criteria.[38] So in anticipation of the judgment seat of Christ, be careful what you say and do in this life. James gives this advice: *So speak and act as those who are to be judged by the law of liberty*" (James 2:12). Jesus cautions us about speaking careless words as we will "*give an accounting for it in the day of judgment*" (Matt. 12:36). Let's have the right motives and character so we can

[37] Romans 14:10 and 2 Corinthians 5:10

[38] Matthew 25:14–30; 1 Corinthians 13:3; Colossians 3:23–24; Hebrews 6:10

give our account with joy on that day. This is why we should strive to serve the Lord faithfully daily.

What the Judgement Seat of Christ is NOT

The judgment seat of Christ does *not* determine your salvation. Your salvation was settled by Christ's sacrifice on your behalf (1 John 2:2) and your faith in Him (John 3:16). As we learned earlier in this book, all our sins are forgiven, and *"there is now no condemnation for those who are in Christ Jesus"* (Rom. 8:1). Jesus said, *"Truly, truly, I say to you, he who hears My word, and believes Him who sent Me, has eternal life, and does not come into judgment, but has passed out of death into life"* (John 5:24).

So, as a believer, you are secure in Christ, but you still must appear before the judgment seat of Christ. It will be a time of examination and a time of reward. Jesus will inspect your works.

The judgment seat of Christ also is *not* a time to punish your sin. Our sins have already been judged at the cross. Jesus took our punishment once and for all nearly two thousand years ago. The judgment seat of Christ is a time when we will be called on to report, to render an accounting of what we did for Jesus. It will be a serious and necessary time of reckoning, but, as God's redeemed, we will never be condemned with the wicked. The judgment seat of Christ is unrelated to the problem of sin, but is a time for the bestowing of rewards.

Jesus is the Judge

Jesus states that He has been given the authority to judge by the Father. In John 5:22-23, Jesus says, *"Not even the Father judges anyone, but He has given all judgment to the Son, so that all will honor the Son even as they honor the Father."* Jesus will act as judge over believers.

At the Bema Seat of Christ, Jesus will judge believers' works after salvation to determine reward or loss of reward.[39] As stated previously, this judgment has nothing to do with salvation, as believers' eternal destiny is secure in Jesus (Eph. 1:13-14). You will receive rewards according to how faithfully you served Christ.[40]

---

[39] I Corinthians 4:5; 2 Corinthians 5:10
[40] Luke 19:12-27; 1 Corinthians 3:12-15; Revelation 22:12

Because Jesus is both God and man, He is the perfect judge of mankind. His judgment will be fair and perfectly just and not subject to appeal (Acts 17:31). He is not like sinful human rulers who at times judge unfairly and seek to fulfill their own agendas. Instead, Jesus stated, *"As I hear, I judge; and My judgement is just, because I do not seek My own will, but the will of Him who sent Me"* (John 5:30*).* You can be assured that Jesus is a fair judge and will enact judgment according to His wisdom and righteousness.

Here is an illustration that summarizes the judgement seat of Christ.

JUDGMENT SEAT OF CHRIST

2 Corinthians 5:10

Who Appears

Only true believers appear

Purpose

-Not to judge salvation
-To evaluate work and motives
-To grant rewards or suffer loss of reward

Basis of Judgment

-Works built on the "foundation" (Christ) are tested by fire
-Enduring works of gold, silver, costly stones = rewards
-Wood, hay, stubble are worthless works = loss of reward, but still saved

Timing & Judge

-Occurs after rapture, before Christ returns in glory
-Christ alone is judge (John 5:22-27)

Heavenly Rewards

The Bible mentions rewards in heaven multiple times.[41] But why are rewards necessary? Won't being in heaven with God be enough? Experiencing Him, His glory, and the joys of heaven will be so wonderful, it's hard to understand why extra rewards would be needed. Also, since our faith rests in Christ's righteousness instead of our own, it may seem strange that our works would merit reward.

[41] Matthew 5:12; Luke 6:23, 35; 1 Corinthians 3:14; 9:19

The Bible says of God that *"He is a rewarder"* (Heb. 11:6). Specifically, the scriptures tell us *"If any man's work which he has built on it* [the foundation of Christ] *remains, he will receive a reward"* (1 Cor. 3:14). Rewards in heaven are a part of your inheritance in Christ as an adopted son or daughter (Col. 3:24). God will give rewards in heaven in order to fulfill the law of sowing and reaping and make good on His promise that our labor in the Lord is not in vain.[42] Any story is not satisfying if it is not completed. Rewards in heaven are the completion of our earthly story, and our rewards will be eternally satisfying (Ps. 16:11).

> Rewards in heaven are a part of your inheritance in Christ as an adopted son or daughter.

Jesus will give rewards in heaven at the *bema*, or the judgment seat of Christ, based on your faithfulness in service to Him. Any rewards or honor you gain in heaven will be precious to you because they carry the weight and meaning of your relationship with God. Rewards are a reminder of what He did through you on earth.

You may be surprised at the small acts of kindness that will be rewarded at the *bema* that are simple expressions of the fruit of the Spirit. Giving a cup of cold water will be rewarded (Matt. 10:42). There seems to be an eternal reward to those who feed the hungry and thirsty, take care of a stranger, cloth the naked, tend to the sick, and visit those in prison (Matt. 25:44-45). Receiving a prophet in the name of a prophet will yield a prophet's reward; receiving a righteous man in the name of a righteous man will yield a righteous man's reward (Matt. 10:41).

The Bible speaks of believers receiving crowns for different things. We believe the judgment seat of Christ is when the crowns will be awarded, and this will take place in heaven soon after the "catching up" of the Church. There are five heavenly crowns mentioned in the New Testament that will be awarded to believers. They are the:

1 - CROWN OF RIGHTEOUSNESS – for Those Who Love the Lord's Appearing

This Crown is for those believers who were ready and waiting for the return of Jesus - all those who love His Appearing. Paul writes, "*In the future, there is laid up for me the crown of righteousness, which the Lord, the righteous Judge, will award to me on that day; and not only to me, but also to all who have loved His appearing*" (2 Tim. 4:8).

---

[42] See Galatians 6:4, 6:7-9; Colossians 3:24; Hebrews 6:10; I Corinthians 15:58

2 – IMPERISHABLE CROWN – for Disciplined Bodies/Self-Control

This is the *Victor's Crown* - for those who disciplined their bodies, and brought their bodies unto subjection— and had self-control. Paul again writes, "*Everyone who competes for the prize is temperate in all things. Now they do it to obtain a perishable crown, but we for an imperishable crown. . . But I discipline my body and bring it into subjection, lest, when I have preached to others, I myself should become disqualified*" (1 Cor. 9:25, 27 NKJV).

3 - CROWN OF LIFE – for Enduring Patiently through Trials

This is the *Martyr's Crown* - for those who were faithful unto death -- those who patiently endured testing, temptations, and trials. James writes, "*Blessed is a man who perseveres under trial; for once he has been approved, he will receive the crown of life which the Lord has promised to those who love Him*" (James 1:12). In the book of Revelation, John wrote to a persecuted church in Smyrna, "*Do not fear what you are about to suffer. . .you will be tested. Be faithful until death, and I will give you the crown of life*" (Rev. 2:10)

Other scriptures that point to the reward for suffering (being hated, insulted, and scorned for the Kingdom) include Matthew 5:12 and Luke 6:22-23. In addition, there is a great reward for loving your enemies (Luke 6:35).

4 - CROWN OF REJOICING – for Winning Souls

This is the *Soul Winner's Crown* - For believers who were obeying Jesus' Great Commission. The apostle Paul writes that "*For if I preach the gospel. . .I have a reward*" (1 Cor. 9:16-17). He writes to the Thessalonians, "F*or what is our hope, or joy, or crown of rejoicing? Is it not even you in the presence of our Lord Jesus Christ at His coming? For you are our glory and joy*" (1 Thess. 2:19-20 NKJV). Those who lead many to righteousness will shine like the stars forever and ever (Dan. 12:3).

5 - CROWN OF GLORY – for Godly Leaders who are Examples to the Flock

This is the Elder's Crown for those leaders, pastors, elders, prophets, apostles, and teachers who were godly examples to the flock of believers that were entrusted and assigned to their care. The apostle Peter writes to leaders:

"Shepherd the flock of God among you, exercising oversight. . .proving to be examples to the flock. And when the Chief Shepherd appears, you will receive the unfading crown of glory" (I Peter 5:2)

At the very end of the Bible, Jesus said, *"Behold, I am coming quickly, and My reward is with Me, to render to every man according to what he has done"* (Rev. 22:12).

Let's Discuss!

In preparation for the judgment seat of Christ, what are you choosing to "build" with? Are you choosing to build with things that last -- gold, silver, and precious stones?

It's Party Time!

After the rewards are given, it will be time to party! We will be ushered into the marriage supper of the Lamb. Revelation 19:7 and 9 records:

> *"Let us rejoice and be glad and give glory to Him, for the marriage of the Lamb has come and His bride has made herself ready.*
>
> *Then he said to me, 'Write, "Blessed are those who are invited to the marriage supper of the Lamb."*

Let's Internalize and Apply!

1. When does the first resurrection begin and when does it conclude?

   ____

   ____

2. True/False: Those who take part in the first resurrection will go to the Great White Throne Judgment.

3. True/False: The Judgment Seat of Christ does not determine our salvation but does determine the rewards believers will receive.

4. True/False: The judgment seat of Christ is *not* a time to punish your sin but to bestow rewards.

5. Who will serve as the Judge at the Judgment Seat of Christ?

____

____

6. What will Jesus give in heaven at the *bema*, or the judgment seat of Christ?

____

____

7. True/False: You can be assured that Jesus is a fair judge and will enact judgment according to His wisdom and righteousness.

8. The scripture mentions crowns as a specific kind of a reward. What are the five crowns mentioned in scripture?

____

____

Chapter 23

Judgment of the Unjust

We have come to the judgment of the unjust or unrighteous ones who refused to believe in the Lord Jesus Christ to be their Savior. It is referred to as the final judgment or the last judgment. Why the last judgment? Well, the Judgement Seat of Christ of all believers has occurred. Also, the beast and the false prophet were judged and thrown into the lake of fire which burns with brimstone (Rev. 19:20). And Satan, the devil and deceiver, has just been judged and thrown into the lake of fire and brimstone to be tormented day and night (Rev. 20:10). Now the final judgment must occur -- the unsaved of all history, both small and great.

This judgment is called the Great White Throne Judgment. The destiny of the unsaved is the lake of fire which is so unfortunate because the lake of fire was only prepared for the devil and his fallen angels (Matt. 25:41). This judgment is where the punishment of the unjust ones is pronounced.

This judgment is only for those in the second resurrection -- the unjust or unrighteous. (Recall that all Christian believers were in the first resurrection and were rewarded at the Judgment Seat of Christ.) This final judgment, however, takes place at the end of the one-thousand-year millennial reign of Christ on the earth.

The Great White Throne Judgment

The great white throne judgment is the final judgment prior to the lost being cast into the lake of fire. Revelation 20:11-15 describes this clearly:

> *Then I saw a great white throne and Him who sat upon it, from whose presence earth and heaven fled away, and no place was found for them.*
> *And I saw the dead, the great and the small, standing before the throne, and books were opened; and another book was opened, which is the book of life; and the dead were judged from the things which were written in the books, according to their deeds.*

> *And the sea gave up the dead which were in it, and death and Hades gave up the dead which were in them; and they were judged, every one of them according to their deeds.*
> *Then death and Hades were thrown into the lake of fire. This is the second death, the lake of fire.*
> *And if anyone's name was not found written in the book of life, he was thrown into the lake of fire.*

This remarkable passage describes the final judgment—the end of history and the beginning of the eternal state of the unjust. The unrighteous will stand before Christ, who will judge them based on two criteria: (1) their works and (2) the Book of Life.

The books that "*were opened*" are probably a record of their lives. God will judge everyone according to his or her soul's condition and the works done in the body. God knows everything that has ever been said, done, or even thought, and He will reward or punish each one accordingly.[43] The apostle Paul writes that unbelievers are currently storing up wrath against themselves and that God "*will render to each person according to his deeds*" (Rom. 2:5-6).

Also at this time, another book is opened, called the "*book of life.*" It is this book that determines whether a person will inherit eternal life with God or receive everlasting punishment in the lake of fire. The dead, referring to the unjust, will be judged "*according to their deeds*" and if "*anyone's name*" is "*not found written in the book of life*" they will be "*thrown into the lake of fire*" (Rev. 20:15). Those whose names are not in the book of life will be judged according to their deeds to determine the degree of punishment they will receive in the lake of fire.

Revelation 20:14 concludes this section by recording, "*Then death and Hades were thrown into the lake of fire. This is the second death, the lake of fire.*"

The Righteous Judge

Jesus Christ is the Judge seated on the Great White Throne. The apostle Paul told those in Athens that "*He* [the Father] *has fixed a day in which He will judge the world in righteousness through a Man* [Christ] *whom He has appointed, having furnished proof to*

[43] See Psalm 28:4; 62:12; Romans 2:5-6; Revelation 2:23; 18:6; 22:12

all men by raising Him from the dead (Acts 17:31). Even Jesus himself said, *"Not even the Father judges anyone, but He has given all judgment to the Son, so that all will honor the Son even as they honor the Father"* (John 5:22–23).

So Jesus Christ is not only the judge of believers at the *Bema* or the Judgement Seat of Christ, but He is also the judge of the unjust at the Great White Throne Judgment.

Here is an illustration that summarizes the White Throne Judgement.

WHITE THRONE JUDGMENT
Revelation 20:11-15

Who Appears
-Only the unjust or unrighteous

Purpose
-To judge the works and motives of the unjust

Basis of Judgment
-To pronounce eternal judgments based on their works and absence of name in Book of Life

Timing & Judge
-At end of time after Beast, False Prophet, and Satan thrown into Lake of Fire
-Christ alone is judge (John 5:22-27)

Eternal Punishment

The lake of fire will be worse than we can imagine—a place of regret and terrible suffering. It will be the eternal dwelling of all who reject Jesus as Savior. *"The lake of fire is the second death"* (Rev. 20:14). Those who experience this second death will be separated from God forever. They will suffer for eternity.

The Bible is careful to let us know that the final destiny of the lost is terrible beyond imagination. It will involve tribulation, anguish, weeping, and gnashing of teeth. It is a furnace of fire and brimstone, causing eternal loss, or everlasting destruction. Its fires, by their very nature, will be unquenchable, and the smoke of their torment will go up forever and ever, so they will have no rest. No wonder the Bible says it is a fearful thing to fall into the hands of the living God.[44]

God does not want anyone to die without Christ; He desires that all would repent and be saved by grace through faith (2 Pet. 3:9). Yet He will not wait forever. He gives us the freedom to choose whether to accept or reject Him. Making the choice to reject Him leads to eternal despair and suffering. Believe us, you don't ever want to end up there. Accepting Him brings us everlasting life.

Have you received Jesus Christ as your Savior yet? If not, now is the right time to do so. Pray with us:

> "Heavenly Father, thank you for sending your Son, the Lord Jesus Christ, to die for my sins that I may have eternal life and spend eternity with you. I believe that Jesus Christ is the Son of God. I repent of all my sins and I ask You to forgive me of all unrighteousness.
>
> Jesus I invite you now to come into my heart and be my Savior. I want to live my life now in obedience to you. Thank you for coming into my heart and making me a new creation in Christ. In Jesus Name, amen."

Let's Internalize and Apply!

1. What judgments will occur before the last judgment, the Great White Throne Judgment?

   ____

   ____

2. The last judgment is only for those in the second resurrection. Who does this include?

   ____

   ____

---

[44] See Matthew 13:42, 50; 22:13; 25:30; Romans 2:9; 2 Thessalonians 1:9; Mark 9:43; Revelation 14:11; 20:10; Hebrews 10:31

3. The unrighteous will stand before Christ, who will judge them based on what two criteria?

____

____

4. Who will serve as the Judge at the Great White Throne Judgment?

____

____

5. After the unjust are judged, what does Revelation 20:14 tell us that will also be thrown into the lake of fire?

____

____

Appendix A: Answers to Internalize & Apply Questions

Chapter 1: Becoming a Mature Son

1. The word *perfection* in Hebrews 6:1 means a state of being mature or complete. A fully mature person possesses full authority to represent the family name and business.
2. The Greek word *huios* is a fully matured "son."
3. The term *huiothesia* means "placed" into "sonship." In the case of Christ, the *huiothesia* ceremony positioned him as a mature "son." The Father is telling you, "You are My beloved Son (*huios)*, in You I am well-pleased."
4. True.
5. True.
6. True.
7. The spiritual battle we are a part of has always been between "the sons" -- the sons of light and the sons of darkness.

Chapter 2 – One Version of You

1. The Father only sees you as a new creation in Christ, your new man.
2. Because you are co-identified with Christ, your old nature was left in the grave.
3. The Father only deals with your new man because He killed off your old man on the cross and left it in the grace.

Chapter 3 – Not Modifiable

1. The Father treats you like He treats Jesus.
2. You are seeking to resurrect your old nature that Jesus killed off at the cross. You are responding from your flesh rather than your born-again spirit.
3. Modifying your behavior seeks to modify your old nature. Instead, the Father gave you a new Christ nature and now reprograms your mind with the mind of Christ to reflect the ways of the new man.
4. True.

Chapter 5 – Jesus in the Mirror

1. I AM factor: your I AM-ness from God; how the Father made you and sees you.
2. I Am imposter: an inaccurate understanding of who you are as a Christian.
3. Move to I AM factor by reading God's Word to accurately understand who you are in your born-again spirit, and speak it with your mouth.
4. God the Father has the exclusive right to assign a name to me. I should respond by wearing the name that I have been given from my Creator.

Chapter 6 – What's True About the One Version of You

1. My born-again spirit is the 'real me'.
2. God sees my born-again spirit that is as righteous, holy, perfect, and complete as Jesus. My born-again spirit is as perfect as it will be in eternity.
3. Sin-consciousness: see self as still a sinner at my core; Righteousness consciousness: see self (my identify) as righteous, holy, perfect, and complete as Jesus
4. No, your born-again spirit does not participate in sin and, in fact, is not capable of committing sin.
5. True.
6. True.

Chapter 7: Winning in the Courtroom of Heaven

1. True.
2. The Courts of Heaven are located in the third heaven where God resides.
3. True.
4. True.
5. True.
6. Jesus *judges*, then *makes war*. *Judging* is judicial activity in the courtroom of Heaven (i.e., for us, getting favorable verdicts based upon evidence – repenting and apply the blood of Christ) and *waging war* is battlefield activity (i.e., for us, binding and loosing, declarations, decrees).

Chapter 8: Repenting from Dead Works

1. Dead works is the belief that you can earn the Father's love and acceptance through your human efforts, your good works, or your religious traditions. This leaves you with a *sin-consciousness*.
2. You cleanse your conscience of dead works when you repent of this wrong thinking and ask for the blood of Jesus Christ to speak on your behalf in the Courts.

Chapter 9: The Completeness of Forgiveness

1. No, not an issue between you and God now. God the Father accepted the full payment of His Son on the cross for all your sins – past, present, and future.
2. All my sins – past, present and future – have been forgiven.
3. No. Jesus was offered one time to pay for all my sins – past, present, and the ones I will commit in the future.
4. Heaven. I am righteous and holy in my born-again spirit, and all my sins have been paid for once and for all.

Chapter 10 – The Gift of a Good Conscience

1. Devil, or a defiled (untransformed) conscience
2. Dead works view: that God loves me and accepts me based on my performance – my doing. Your conscience is cleansed from "dead works" when you fully accept that Christ's full payment for your sins is what makes you accepted to the Father.
3. An evil conscience is the erroneous belief that your core self (your spirit) as a Christian is still sinful in some way. It's still thinking that there are two versions of you: your new nature and your old nature. You still have a *sin-consciousness* rather than a *righteousness-consciousness*. You will need to reprogram your conscience by repenting of continuing to believe there are two versions of you and believe the truth that God only sees one version of you – the new man.
4. No, your born-again spirit is as holy, clean, pure, and perfect as Jesus. Your spirit is as perfect and complete as it will ever be.

Chapter 11 – "Give Me Back My Stuff"

1. True.
2. No, negativity is a part of your old man, or sin nature.
3. All of your sins and negativity in all its forms – negative thinking, negative behavior, negative emotions, sarcasm, and cynicism.
4. All negativity is an assault against your identity in Christ, distract from your true identity and destiny, distort how you perceive who you really are in Christ, and challenge the truths God has declared about you.
5. The areas are your *perception* of what's true in your born-again spirit, how you *think* and *feel* about yourself, and how you *talk* about yourself.
6. Attachments come from such sources as the flesh, the world system, and religion.
7. Change the thought to a truth or promise and work on that new thought. Religion tells you to work on the negative thought.
8. True.

Chapter 12: Faith in God

1. God the Father, who is the Judge of all, is for you as He delivered up his Son for you. Jesus is also for you as He died and shed His blood for you. He is also at the right hand of the Father always interceding for you as your advocate and defense attorney.
2. Jesus' shed blood *"speaks better things"* about you in the courts of Heaven and answers every accusation against you.
3. True.
4. First, Christ rescued you from sin by *redeeming* you with His own precious blood. Second, Jesus satisfied the Father's righteous anger, wrath, and fiery indignation against all of your sins and turned aside the Father's wrath forever (known as *propitiation*). As a result of this, the Father is right in *justifying* you.
5. False.

6. True.

Chapter 14: The Recircuiting Process

1. What **lie** am I believing about my identity? What's **true** about my identity?
2. Rejecting and Renouncing the lie followed by Declaring and Announcing what is scripturally true to form a new agreement.

Chapter 15: Baptized Into Christ

1. When you receive Jesus Christ as your Savior, the Holy Spirit does the baptizing, and He places you into the Body of Christ, the Church.
2. You received three other elements as a part of the salvation "package": the fullness of the Godhead, the authority of the believer, and the fruit of the Spirit.
3. You receive *authority* as part of the new birth, when you receive Jesus Christ as your Savior. John 1:12-13 is a clear scripture that associates your authority as a believer as a part of the new birth.
4. The basis of your authority in Christ is your close co-identity with the finished work of Christ in His crucifixion, burial, resurrection, ascension, and seating.
5. The fruit of the Spirit was imparted into your spirit in *seed* form when you were *born* of the Spirit. The fruit were planted in your life as nine different *seeds* that are to be watered and cultivated until they grow to maturity.

Chapter 16: Baptized into Water

1. Baptism by immersion in water illustrates your identification with Christ's death, burial, and resurrection.
2. When you are baptized in water, you are publicly declaring that you are dead to your sin nature and alive unto God.
3. When you are raised out of the water, you are symbolically resurrected—raised to new life in Christ to be with Him forever. It illustrates Christ's resurrection.
4. Baptism, by its inherent definition, must be an act of immersion in water.
5. Any two of the following: Water baptism is commanded by Jesus; Water baptism publicly expresses turning away from your old nature and an embracing your new nature; Water baptism circumcises your heart; Water baptism expresses obedience and love for our Lord Jesus; Water baptism expresses unity with all the saints.

Chapter 17: Baptism in the Holy Spirit

1. The Scripture clearly identifies Jesus Christ, the Anointed One, as the person of the Godhead who baptizes or immerses you in the Holy Spirit.
2. You are baptized into the fullness of the Holy Spirit.
3. The Holy Spirit proceeds to us from the Father through Jesus Christ the Son.
4. False.

5. The initial sign or physical evidence of the baptism in the Holy Spirit is speaking in tongues.
6. True.

Chapter 18: Laying on of Hands

1. The principle of laying on of hands is the belief and scriptural practice that spiritual power or qualities can be transferred from one believer to another by laying one's hands upon that individual.
2. You can impart the Holy Spirit and spiritual gifts, healing to the sick, install leaders, or bless and strengthen others as you lay your hands upon them and pray.
3. True.
4. True.
5. Strengthening effect.
6. True.

Chapter 19: The Resurrection of the Righteous

1. False. The first resurrection is the raising of the *physical* bodies of all believers.
2. The first stage of the first resurrection was the resurrection of Jesus Christ.
3. True.
4. Jesus Christ will be the judge of believers at the Judgment Seat of Christ.
5. True.
6. True.
7. Our new spiritual body will have a continuing identification with the old physical body, we will still be individuals in our new bodies, and our new bodies will be perfect.
8. The third stage of the first resurrection is the resurrection of the martyrs.
9. True.

Chapter 20: Eternal State of the Believer

1. True.
2. True.
3. Yes, in heaven we will know our friends and family members, and will be known by them.
4. True.

Chapter 21: Resurrection of the Unjust

1. The second resurrection is the raising of all unbelievers, those whose names are not found in the "book of life."
2. Those summoned to the second resurrection are the wicked who are (1) judged at the great white throne judgment prior to (2) being cast into the lake of fire.
3. True.
4. False: The second resurrection will occur at the end of Christ's millennial reign.
5. Today, the unrighteous dead remain in *Sheol* (*Hades* in Greek) until the time of the second resurrection. It is an interim place of waiting, and is also called Abraham's bosom.

Chapter 22: Judgment of the Righteous

1. The first resurrection will begin with the "catching up" of the Church and end with the resurrection of the Tribulation martyrs.
2. False: They will go to the Judgment Seat of Christ.
3. True.
4. True.
5. Jesus will serve as the Judge as the Father has given the authority to judge to Christ.
6. Jesus will judge believers' works to determine reward or loss of reward, according to how faithfully you served Christ.
7. True.
8. The five crowns are: Crown of Life, Crown of Righteousness, Crown of Glory, Crown of Rejoicing, and the Imperishable Crown.

Chapter 23: Judgment of the Unjust

1. The judgment that will occur prior to the Great White Throne Judgment will be the Judgment Seat of Christ, and the judgment against the beast, false prophet, and the Devil where they are thrown into the lake of fire.
2. The last judgment is for those who are unjust or unrighteous across all ages of time.
3. The two criteria are: the works of the unjust and the Book of Life. The books are probably a record of their lives. God will judge everyone according to his or her soul's condition and the works done in the body. God knows everything that has ever been said, done, or even thought, and He will reward or punish each one accordingly
4. Christ the King will serve as the judge at the Great White Throne Judgment.
5. Revelation 20:14 tells us that death and Hades will be thrown into the lake of fire. This is the second death, the lake of fire.

About the Authors

Dr. Lon Stettler is an ordained minister and educator who is very passionate about discipleship and maturity. He has been very active in the discipleship ministry for over four decades. Lon has written, preached, and taught discipleship courses for more than thirty years. He holds a Doctor of Philosophy degree from Miami University in educational leadership and served as a school district administrator for 26 years.

Laurie is a mother of four children and retired high school teacher who enjoys crocheting and time with family. Laurie and Lon have seven wonderful grandchildren.

Lon and Laurie currently live near Charleston, South Carolina. Contact:
lon.stettler@gmail.com or lonstettler.com

About the Authors

www.ingramcontent.com/pod-product-compliance
Lightning Source LLC
LaVergne TN
LVHW081318110826
845149LV00006B/1539

* 9 7 9 8 9 9 3 6 4 7 8 0 7 *